THE RETAIL EXPERIMENT

Five Proven Strategies to Engage & Excite Customers Through In-Store Experience

AMY ROCHE

'Amy's fun approach to retail today is insightful, carefully considered and comes from real-world experiences that any retail executive or manager could implement. She demystifies abstract ideas and links them back to human behaviour with practical and actionable advice for making stores more exciting for shoppers.'

David Woollcott, CEO Winning Appliances

'*The Retail Experiment* is exactly that: an experiment to identify the successes and pitfalls of the customer experience based on real-life tests. As with all experiments, sometimes the results were unexpected. Amy has done the hard yards to develop insightful, relevant and implementable strategies for retailers using her own store as the lab.'

Oliver Ranck, CEO Octomedia, publisher of *Inside Retail*

'In today's world it simply isn't enough any more to just provide good products with great service. Your clients are wanting more; no – they are *demanding* more. They are wanting an amazing experience when they walk through your door. *The Retail Experiment* couldn't come at a better time. Experience works in retail, and this book is full of great ideas and strategies that will engage your very best customers, reduce competition and increase profit.'

Karl Schwantes, Managing Director, Xennox Diamonds

'There are very few people in the world of retail that understand just how important the customer experience actually is. Amy Roche is one of those people. If I was a retailer, she is the only person I would call to help me create an in-store experience that translates to sales every time.'

Andrew Griffiths, International Bestselling Business Author, Speaker and Commentator

'The retail landscape is changing rapidly and Amy's passion for re-writing customer experience couldn't come at a better time for both customers and retailers.

'I've seen first-hand how Amy's in-store events engaged my customers. Her success, ideas and proactive strategy ensure a deeper client connection that pure online businesses would be challenged to compete with.'

Previous client & former owner, James Brockhurst, The Good Guys, Capalaba

'The market has changed. Customers don't just want your product, or good customer service, they want a "retail experience"! Amy is a thought leader and a change-maker in this area. If you are in retail, at the very least, you need to read her book!'

Lisa Cutforth, Owner of Fit Foods Club & Healthy Meals to Your Door

'I love working with Amy. The conversations, the ideas and the professionalism in every event I've been part of, I've been lucky to be a Retail Rockstar with Amy and I would love to be part of that experience again because Amy made it so easy. Everyone from the attendees to the clients were happy, and even the smallest details were taken care of. I love everything Amy does.'

Ronsley Vaz, Chief Day Dreamer, AMPLIFY

Book production by
Michael Hanrahan Publishing
PO Box 319
Surrey Hills, Vic. 3127
http://mhpublishing.com.au

First published in 2017 by Amy Roche

National Library of Australia Cataloguing-in-Publication entry:

Creator: Roche, Amy, author.
Title: The retail experiment.
ISBN: 9781925648294 (paperback).
Subjects: Retail trade.
Retail trade – Customer services.
Sales management.
Consumer profiling.
Customer services – Management.

Text design by Michael Hanrahan Publishing
Cover design by Lauren Jennings

Disclaimer
The material in this publication is of the nature of general comment only, and does not represent professional advice. It is not intended to provide specific guidance for particular circumstances and it should not be relied on as the basis for any decision to take action or not take action on any matter which it covers. Readers should obtain professional advice where appropriate, before making any such decision. To the maximum extent permitted by law, the author and publisher disclaim all responsibility and liability to any person, arising directly or indirectly from any person taking or not taking action based on the information in this publication.

CONTENTS

PART III BECOMING MORE THAN A SALES MACHINE

PART IV MOVE OVER, ARNOLD … WE'RE TALKIN' HUMANICS

PART V SAY WHAT? SAY EXPERIENTIAL RETAILING

STRATEGY THREE: EXPERIENTIAL RETAILING

PART VI RETAIL STORYTELLING AND A GOOD NARRATIVE

STRATEGY FOUR: RETAIL STORYTELLING

PART VII EVENTS: BEST-KEPT SECRET FOR RETAIL

STRATEGY FIVE: IN-STORE EVENTS

WELCOME TO THE RETAIL EXPERIMENT

As someone who has owned a successful retail store as well as headed up global and national marketing for twenty years, I know what a retailer's life is like these days. Despite spending more and more on clever marketing, you probably feel like your customers are listening to you less and less. Not that long ago, you'd activate an advertising campaign and then brace yourself for the wave of people and sales. You'd see a fairly big reaction in terms of increased visitation to the store and a spike in sales too. Who would have thought these curves and spikes would wane in such a short period of time? No doubt you're wondering what has changed so dramatically since then.

Your days as a retailer get crazier and crazier with staff demands and plenty of let-downs too. You are constantly being bombarded with angrier and more demanding customers, day by day. And each year small increments of profit are eroded through online sales and increased global competition. As staff leave and uncertainty sets in, you slowly stop replacing staff – meaning you feel the squeeze when people need to take holidays.

Despite all of this, you're still investing in the latest retail technology and marketing campaigns and, if you're part of a franchise or corporate outfit, you'll also have an ambassador or cause program to add pressure to your P&L.

You've been generous with customers, giving them bigger and bigger discounts, loyalty cards, the best-trained staff and helpful emails and you wonder – what more could these customers possibly want from me?

EXPERIMENTING

So how close am I? Believe me, I know the drill. As I said, I've been in the marketing and retail industry for twenty years, and for the last eleven years, I've owned a 2500m² appliance store. I've seriously been there. Although we were operating in the top quarter of the 109 stores across Australia, I could see our customers were starting to react differently to our marketing campaigns. In fact, I was so frustrated at their lack of interest, I started 'experiments' in my own store to find some answers to these changing consumer behaviours and to solve the mystery of why customers were drifting away.

Of course, I'm not talking about beakers and test tubes here. Mine was more of a social experiment to uncover why customers were getting more distrustful and fickle – why they were so disengaged? Why, after getting amazing service, great pricing, range and knowledgeable staff, were they driving around to 10 different businesses for the best price when we were all within $10 of each other? Why, when we had a massive sale with our best prices ever, did we have fewer and fewer people coming through the front door?

In the end, I worked out it doesn't have to be this way. Just like the entrepreneurial movement has discovered, price doesn't rule customers. They are engaged by extremely helpful and personal messages and gestures. If we inspire them, educate them and help them live better lives, they will remember us – and our stores.

Engaging your customers is relatively easy and straightforward to do in your store. It doesn't take several million dollars, a branding or customer experience consultant or approval from head office (if you have one). What it does take is a bit of courage to let go of what you think it means to be a retailer – moving away from a focus on selling your wares in the most productive and cost-effective manner, to genuinely wanting to engage and provide experiences with your customers. The rest is a piece a cake and not that costly if you're prepared to look at your retail business in a different light and put aside a bit of extra time and money for connecting with people on a person-to-person level.

Instead of thinking big, think smaller (regardless of how big you are). Instead of thinking generic, think personalised; instead of thinking national, think like a local. Above all, recognise that humans trump all interactions and experiences. Real connection and change come from humans with a shared cause and sense of community.

BEATING AMAZON AND BEING A BIT 'WOO-WOO'

Now, I know you likely think this is all a bit 'woo-woo' sounding … and, frankly, when I stumbled on these strategies I was thinking, *Surely I'm missing something here.* I wondered how these things were going to help when I was competing against bigger retailers locally – or, even worse yet, Amazon. As I was going about my research, I uncovered recurring topics, and some of the ideas had even been starting to work for me in-store – ideas like experiential retailing, events, localisation, humanics and retail storytelling. But even as these theories kept popping up, and I'd seen some success from them in-store, I was still cynical about how these would help improve my profit, increase sales, visitation and loyalty. And, above all, how in the world can they break through to these customers that I've been spending bucket loads already to reach and, frankly, don't seem to give a damn?

Prior to being a retailer, I was a global marketing manager and before that was a marketing manager at Maytag, a Fortune 500 company in the US. So, my first inclination from my previous knowledge in marketing was to assume any successes I'd seen in engaging customers must have come down to the magic of the expert I had facilitating an event, or the marketing copy of an offer or experience. But after testing different combinations and reviewing results what I realised was that it was indeed a combination of all the strategies I'd uncovered and the sequence in which strategies were completed. Only after experimenting and moving things around did we experience the hugest impact with re-engaging our customers and drawing new like-minded customers to us like magnets.

So this book is the story of how I discovered – through trial and error in our retail store – that profit, sales, visitation and loyalty are intrinsically linked to customer engagement, or lack thereof. It was a discovery that uncovered how the sales campaign mindset is in direct conflict with deep customer engagement. In many ways, *The Retail Experiment* will challenge a seasoned retailer's intuition (which is exactly the point).

Who this book is for

This book is written for my fellow comrades, the retail owners, the franchisees, the joint venture partners, the store managers ... ya know – the real-deal, in-the-midst-of-it-all types of retailers. This is for the person who, like me, turns up every day (okay, most days). It's for the retailer who wants to play a bigger game – certainly, a more rewarding and profitable game, but also a better game. One that involves a less 'icky' salesy way of being successful at retail and that resonates with your absolute best customers.

This book is not for C-suite managers working in head offices who for all their strategies and projections probably don't know the first thing about running a retail store in today's climate – because theory has no place in retail today. Instead, this book is for those

4

who understand the challenges of dealing with real-life customers and staff and turning the lights on every day.

I *love* retail, but I feel … No, let me rephrase that: I *know* that real change comes when leaders inside the store and their customers come face to face. It's this magical connection, or this potential connection, that excites me. I write this book despite all the retail 'gurus' who are spouting off that bricks-and-mortar is dead, and that *all* the problems lie squarely on the shoulders of retailers and their inability to have an 'omnichannel' experience. You have the power to change your store (or stores) and it is here that I'm interested in playing, learning and helping other retailers.

I'm going to go out on a limb here and assume that you probably loved retailing at one time, maybe still do a bit, but it's now become a lot less fun than it used to be. Well, I love retail too – in fact, I've been friends with competitor retailers for years because we all share a common love of retail, having fun with your suppliers and industry (and in general), and we all really do thrive in fast-paced, crazy environments. That's why we are good at what we do – retailing. So it's time to get the love back.

I hope that by sharing *The Retail Experiment*, you'll understand the pitfalls and the real game-changers to help you enjoy and become successful at retailing once again. I'm pretty confident this book will help not only bring back the love you once had for retail, but also get you back on the path to re-engaging your disengaged customers, and then restoring sustainable profit, sales, loyalty and visitation in your store.

How this book is organised

Throughout the book, I share my Retail Experiment journey – outlining what worked along with some pretty big fails too. I share what I observed and implemented, and how my strategies affected our customers and subsequent other retailers as I moved from 'experimentation mode' to helping colleagues and later working with other retailers in my own business.

In the first part of this book, I share some major psychological changes affecting consumer behaviours and how those are playing out for retailers and their marketing and sales models. I then go over the economic value of engagement, highlighting the money you're leaving on the table by not focusing on customer engagement. The next part outlines what we did in our store – that is, the actual 'Retail Experiment'. From there, parts III to VII are dedicated to a detailed look at the five major strategies we used for success within the experiment, covering approaches such as moving past the sales machine, humanics, localisation, retail storytelling, experiential retailing, live events and in-store experiences.

Here's some more detail on what to find in each part:

1   *The new customer and the value of customer engagement:* In this part, you'll find research, observations and information on why consumers are different and why we need to change to meet them. I also throw some numbers around on why you should care so much about engagement, and what it's worth if you get it right.

2   *The experiment:* Finally we get to the guts of my strategies and approaches! Here I run through where we started, what failed, what worked and what we did to make it even better.

3   *Become more than a sales machine:* Humour me – 'sales machine' is my own made-up term, but it has *real* relevance. This part covers the first of our strategies and is all about revealing how we can change to meet our customers.

4   *Humanics:* Focusing on the human side of retail helps you to create strong personal bonds that mean something and build reciprocity. In this part, I also talk about localisation and how to use it to your advantage.

5   *Experiential retailing:* Here you'll get to understand a bit more about what you can do in-store to create experience and excitement and keep people coming back.

6   *Retail storytelling:* Here we dissect a great narrative and see how this strategy can be used as a force multiplier in retail – for customers, staff and suppliers.

7   *Live in-store events:* In this part, I bring together all the main ideas of this book and share the latest info on why events are amazing little re-engagement piñatas – exploding with all kinds of good things for retailers. I also get you ready to start planning your own events.

The book concludes with a summary of the main ideas, and a quick look at where retail might go in the future (and it's looking good).

In each chapter from part III onwards (where we get to the strategies and how you can use them in your store), I will also provide key 'Time out' exercises to get you started on your very own Retail Experiment. Please take the time to review and actually do these activities, discuss them with your team and implement them within your store.

GETTING THE MOST OUT OF *THE RETAIL EXPERIMENT*

Our time-poor society means that not everyone will pick up *The Retail Experiment* and read it from cover to cover. While I've never been a big fan of repeating myself, you'll find I do repeat (or at least summarise) important key phrases and strategies throughout the book to keep the information relevant for those skipping ahead to the strategies that interest them most, or they're most in need of now.

I will say, however, that the Experiment's power lies not so much in the individual strategies, but in the sequence and stacking of all five strategies. This combination is what will affect your figures and bring long-term success to your retail business.

I'm not going to lie: some of the ideas in this book may annoy you. What I mean is that, as retailers, our natural state is that of 'sales mode'. It likely seems counterintuitive to think of giving something such as knowledge or experiences away for free. People come to us to buy things – and our job is to sell them stuff. The initial response from many of my colleagues was, 'What if they don't buy anything?' I've gone to great lengths in part III of this book (where I talk about becoming more than a sales machine) to provide research and demonstrate why this strategy no longer serves us retailers. So what I'm saying is, to get the most out of this book, you must 'lean in' to these somewhat uncomfortable ideas.

Remember – you have the power to change your store, no matter what structures exist above your ownership or management. My inner *Star Wars* warrior says, 'May the force be with you', but I think since you picked up this book, you already know there must be a better way. And there is – a more contemporary way that can not only help your customers but also profoundly affect the communities we trade in. I'd also be crazy not to mention it can produce some wonderful financial results and a whole lot of fun for you and your staff too. So in the famous words of Yoda, 'If no mistake have you made, yet losing you are … a different game you should play.'

Change is the law of life. And those who look only to the past or present are certain to miss the future.

John F Kennedy

Part I

ENGAGING THE NEW CUSTOMER

In this part, we cover three main topics. First off, in chapter 1, we focus on recent psychological and sociological customer research, and how we as retailers need to meet these *new* customers face to face with fresh strategies that appeal to them.

Understanding that you're in retail rather than psychology, I've given you the most up-to-date and compact version of the main trends impacting retailers today. I briefly cover significant changes affecting consumers – things like intense emotions, technology, isolation, the rise of distrust and growing narcissism – and start to consider how we as retailers can reverse-engineer our environments and strategies to build trust and loyalty, and form closer and more profitable bonds with our customers.

Chapter 2 covers the transformation of retail space, providing help with your physical in-store atmosphere while acknowledging that online shopping has profoundly affected customer visitation, in-store browsing and the overall ambience of stores. Here I outline how to give this *new* customer the elements they crave – through aspects like multitasking, simplicity, personalisation, humanistic traits and capitalising on your unique involvement. And we dive into the importance of not only adapting your in-store atmosphere to attract customers but also actually engineering it for a positive psychological experience.

By around chapter 3, you might be asking, 'Even if I can get this customer engagement thing right, what do I stand to gain out of it all?' This is exactly the question I had myself. So I've positioned the answer to this question early (in chapter 3) and kept it short and sweet – because the numbers speak for themselves. In my quest to re-engage my customers, what I outline in this chapter were the first bits of information and research I found. This is what drove me to find a way to make the strategies work specifically for retailers. It's what drove me to experiment in my own store – to bomb out, to fail, to get better and finally to see with my own eyes what engagement can do and how it can transform just about every aspect of your store. I dare to say, if I hadn't found the *value* in what highly engaged customers could do for me, I might not have been so passionate about solving the 'dis-engagement' issue with my customers to begin with.

Personally, I found changing my mindset from *dollars* per square metre to *experience* per square meter challenging. However, the strategies developed through the following parts in this book will help you ease into it. Producing the very best experience for your customers will bring them back time and time again, and will also attract a new, more engaged, loyal and profitable customer for you.

UNDERSTANDING THE NEW CUSTOMER

1

Today one thing is certain: our customers (and ourselves) are savvy and way more narcissistic. It's true; unfortunately, we trust less, and we think way more about ourselves than at any previous time in history. So, it's not really a surprise that this is the so-called Age of the Consumer, is it?

Over the years, I've noticed how our customers have changed. Something that was once appreciated is now adored; what was once slightly aggravating now thoroughly angers them. Consumers today are more vocal, more emotional and way more demanding.

You've probably noticed this play out in your store too. People are getting frustrated and angered very quickly, and the smallest

> Progress is impossible without change, and those who cannot change their minds cannot change anything.
>
> *George Bernard Shaw*

inconveniences turn into major dramas. Even the slightest amount of delay in, well, *anything* can set someone off.

Do you ever wonder who to blame? Are your staff inciting this type of behaviour, or are your customers just turning into a bunch of jerks? The funny thing is, it's a bit of both really. Not only are your customers changing but you and your staff are changing too – at an alarming rate.

INTENSE EMOTIONS: RISE OF STRESS AND ANXIETY IN CUSTOMERS

Yup, you heard me right – your staff and customers are changing at an alarming rate. For example:

- In any 12-month period, approximately 14 per cent of all Australians are affected by an anxiety disorder.[1]

- One in five people worldwide has recently reported increased anger and sadness, with one in three reporting stress or worry.[2]

- In Australia, 35 per cent of people report a significant level of distress in their lives.[3]

- Over 20 per cent of Americans take medications to improve their mental health.

- A 1994 survey of randomly selected households found that 15 per cent of Americans had experienced elevated anxiety the previous year. Sixteen years later this rate has risen to over 49.5 per cent.[4]

Statistics may differ from country to country, but intense and uncomfortable emotions are on the rise everywhere, and understanding customers' emotions and moods is critical for retailers. We now know emotions have a profound impact on not only how we see the world but also how we perceive products and retailers, and therefore these emotions directly affect why and how people shop and buy.

On the positive side, though, elevated levels of anxiety and anger also give people new reasons for buying – not in an icky sort of way, but more in a soothing, taking yourself to the movies kind of way. While our brains do compare value and functional benefits, and weigh up overall choices, our emotions play a large role in what we end up deciding and acting upon.

Recent brain imaging shows that both your 'worrying and computing' centre and your emotional centre are located in the same area of the brain (the ventromedial pre-frontal cortex). That means that when you are worrying about a purchase and computing value for money, the very same part of your brain is also a hotbed of emotions. This proves something smart retailers and marketers have known all along – that emotions enter and play a significant role in the appraisal and trade-off functions of buying decisions.[5]

When underlying emotions burst out

As with all things, many times what plays out in-store as crazy anger is just a case of this massive underlying anxiety mixed with poor judgement.

Let me give you an example. When I still owned my store, I heard someone getting thunderous by our front counter, so naturally, I quickly made my way to the front to see what was going on. Once there, I found a woman, let's call her Sally, who looked around 25 years old. She was extremely upset and very verbose about a $10 hair straightener that didn't work. She said it only lasted five days and then just stopped working, and she wanted to return it (she may have used other, more colourful words than that).

She was getting distraught and, as my staff stared at her in disbelief over how she was reacting to the death of the cheapest hair straightener we sold, she got even worse. We were ready to give her a new straightener, but our staff couldn't get a word in edgewise. I quickly took Sally into my office to continue the conversation where fewer customers were listening, in the hope that she would calm down.

As I talked more to Sally, I found she was upset because she had an interview that morning for what she called her dream job. Unfortunately, at the time she was living with her friend due to a recent redundancy at her last job. She had been tirelessly working to support herself and her son since her ex-partner had left and, as she said, 'This was my one shot'. Jeez, I got a little more than I bargained for on this occasion but, as Sally sat there sobbing at my desk, I couldn't help but feel for her and comfort her.

It was evident to me that she had lost the plot with our staff because she was so frustrated and stressed out over everything else going on in her life. The cheap hair straightener that didn't work was just the last straw in a series of things that had gone wrong that day, that week and really that year. And if she had walked out in that state, I think she would have blamed us for not getting the job.

Now, I know what you are thinking: *What, we're supposed to be psychologists to our customers now?* No, of course not, and I don't normally get this involved either. But we do need to recognise that our dog-eat-dog world does stress people out – to extreme states. Once in these states, they do and say things they normally wouldn't.

And this doesn't just affect your customers. To add another element to what was already a full-blown story, Jan, our customer service person who handled all of our returns – and was the most upbeat woman of all time – had had a pretty crap morning as well. Indeed, she had just been sworn at over the phone and had been fighting with the manufacturer of those *very same* cheap hair straighteners for three weeks to accept our returns. Under normal circumstances, I have no doubt she would have wooed Sally over, but on that day she was a bit flat due to her own issues and the reminder that the company we were still dealing with had yet another faulty product for her to fix up.

After talking with Sally, I realised she was clearly an educated and nice person. I explained the warranty, and said I'd be happy to give her a new unit. I also clarified that I understood her situation, but didn't appreciate her taking out her frustration on my staff. She agreed, apologised profusely to Jan and everyone else and left with a smile on her face, thanking us all for our help.

I share this story because it's one in a million other retail stories, right? As owners and managers, we don't get involved in all the stories that play out throughout the day – let alone all the grumpy-bums that our lovely 'Jans' have served and soothed throughout the years. But I think this story also highlights the rise in irritability we're experiencing in our customers. And recent studies confirm that we do act differently when shopping while stressed and irritable.

In normal circumstances, in other words, when we are not stressed, we primarily use our hippocampus, which is associated with making conscious, deliberate and logical decisions. However, even when we are slightly stressed these mechanisms are thrown out the window.

Another example of this came up in my research – when staff at US-based high-end cookware and kitchen accessories store Williams-Sonoma placed a $429 breadmaker near a $279 model, they didn't sell many of the more expensive breadmakers. However, they sold double the number of the $279 model than usual.[6] This unit had always been the same price, but when placed next to the $429 unit the $279 unit seemed like a real bargain to stressed-out shoppers.

SHOPPERS' STRESS LEVELS AFFECT PURCHASES

Beyond the added stresses of life and not having the time or inclination to check prices or calculate a 30 per cent discount, other less obvious behaviours that deeply impact purchasing for stressed-out shoppers today. As outlined by consumer psychologist Kit Yarrow in *Decoding the New Consumer Mind*[7] these behaviours include the following:

• Shoppers rely more heavily on trusted experts, such as bloggers, cooking programs, friends, social sites or favourite stores that will curate excessive options for them.

- They rely more on in-store feelings to make decisions, so they are less logical and deliberate in decision-making.

- They seek human connection as an antidote for emotional distress (this will be covered in more detail in subsequent chapters).

- They are highly sensitive to complexity – if it's not simple, they are not buying. Likewise, they feel grateful and are loyal to retailers that organise and simplify the buying process for them.

- They are more prone to inertia – buying the same thing without thinking, or just not buying at all if it involves too much change.

- They are more likely to rationalise impulsive purchases. I mean, come on, who hasn't used the phrase, 'it would have cost more for me not to have bought those shoes'? This behaviour and rationalisation can be good if it's in your store, but not good if you are hoping for customers to switch from other retailers to you.

Take one tablet of control, then call me in the morning

Even anxiety, the close brother of stress, puts customers on high alert. Like its 'bro', a bit of anxiety serves to keep us safe, preparing us for that all-important 'fight or flight' mode. But Australia's Heart Foundation, and many other health organisations and practitioners warns us that prolonged anxiety can cause very negative health issues.

A retailer's 'prescription' for anxiety is control. When customers feel they have some control – even the smallest amount – they will feel less anxious. When they are less anxious, they spend more time in your store – and they also remember the positive and calm (that is, not anxious) feeling they had there. As we know, customers spending more time in-store usually means they spend more money, and having a positive psychological experience means they will come back again and again for more positive shopping experiences.

Retailers can help customers feel more in control and less anxious in-store through their verbal language (using phrases like 'it's your decision' and 'you're free to choose') and through taking the hassle out of the selection and knowledge-gathering process. I expand on these ideas throughout the book but, as a taster, great ways to streamline and curate the decision process for customers include events, how-to videos, blogs and online comparisons.

I provide more specific strategies later in this book and, obviously, you're 'free to choose' (wink, wink) which or all that may apply to your own retail environment, but you get the picture. Activating a person's sense of control makes him or her more open to persuasion.[8] This is true because that sense of control sets the anxiety and stress monster at ease. This also links in with why experts and special events featuring experts resonate so well with consumers – and are so powerful for retailers – because they give knowledge and control to the consumer.

Decision-making by committee

In *Decoding the New Consumer Mind*, Kit Yarrow makes a wonderful analogy of how we make purchasing decisions, pointing out that we often have conflicting thoughts and feelings during this process. She refers to the differing viewpoints as the 'customer's committee', arguing:

> One member wants to save money, another is interested in quality, another just wants it to be a fast and an easy decision, another is focused on avoiding guilt – and then there's the fun one who's willing to do what it takes to get an emotional kick. Each committee member is vying for control. But in the purchasing moment, when emotions are in play, Mr Fast and Easy, Ms Fun, and occasionally Dr Guilt have their way.[9]

Ignoring all members in the customer's committee is the problem with traditional market research – and why so many retailers are failing as of late. The majority of retailers are still focusing on the features and benefits or price and product approach. While this 'logical' approach once attracted customers, with higher emotions now in place, it only serves a tiny portion of our customers – those who aren't anxious or emotional or stressed out. I don't know about you, but I'd be eliminated from that mix!

This approach reminds me of one of my favourite scenes from *Ferris Bueller's Day Off* – the one where the teacher is taking role call and keeps calling out 'Bueller, Bueller, Bueller', and no-one answers him. If we keep focusing on the logical side of marketing, like the teacher, no-one will answer our call either. We need to find fresh new ways to incite emotion inside our stores because most customers are already finding the logical features and benefits online, before they ever step foot in-store.

> Without change, there is no innovation, creativity or incentive for improvement. Those who initiate change will have a better opportunity to manage the change that is inevitable.
>
> *William Pollard*

Yes, when asked in focus groups or market research to evaluate products and anticipate what we'll do in the future, we tend to focus on product benefits and characteristics. But in the moment of purchase, we're more likely to shift our attention toward price and are much more responsive to emotional cues.[10]

This is similar to why so many people say eating healthy or being environmentally friendly is their top priority, but a small percentage act in a way that supports those statements. I wouldn't say we flat out lie; it's more that we say what we think we should say or how we would like to act, and not how we will necessarily act.

Soothe highly charged moods and anxiety

In summary, stressed and anxious shoppers can be quite difficult, but only if your store is not specially prepared for them. As retailers, we need to be very mindful of the delicate, anxious and stressed-out states of our customers. We need to have more empathy and to provide our customers with the right elements within our retail environments to make them feel at ease, connected, and to soothe their highly charged moods. Partnering with local trusted experts, providing human connection and simplifying your store to make service and purchasing easier are all ways to soothe anxiety and provide a feeling of control. I'll expand on these options in much greater detail as we progress through the book.

TECHNOLOGY AND OUR BRAINS

We all know that technology has changed us, even if we don't know exactly how. Research now shows our prolific use of technology is physically re-wiring our brains to think differently. It's also changing the way we problem-solve and creating a whole new set of emotional needs by changing our relationships and how we form them. As Kit Yarrow outlines, the cognitive and emotional shifts that result from the use of technology 'have permeated every aspect of our lives and consequently every aspect of HOW and WHY we shop and buy'.[11]

Today, faced with myriad options, consumers will choose or leave retailers because they either help to address the shifts, or fail to recognise them or ignore them.

Technology and innovations to solve all of your problems

Let me give you an example of how people now view technology and other innovations. I owned a vending machine in the foyer of our shop. I know, a crazy decision, but I made it because we were one of the first big tenants at our shopping centre. With no cafes or other big shops around, we needed a quick solution for customers and staff – otherwise, they might leave. While a vending machine is a super-annoying thing to own, maintain and stock, it did give me some great insights into our staff's drinking and snacking habits.

One of our staff, let's call him Mick, was an IT guru. He spent most of his waking hours away from work online – if he wasn't gaming, he was posting YouTube videos of gaming. However, nearly every day he had about four or five energy drinks out of my vending machine. He would stay up most of the night (or so I heard), then come to work a bit tired and in need of some stimulation. It was kinda funny because he also liked wearing a Fitbit, so he'd show his colleagues at work how little sleep he'd had, and then guzzle down some energy drink and cycle through those peaks and troughs throughout the day with coffee and snacks.

Mick told me most of his friends had energy drinks all day and also used other supplements to sleep at night. And they're not alone – rather than listening to their bodies for guidance on when they're tired or awake, Mick and his friends (and many others like them) turn to the marketplace to solve their problems. Whether this solution is a supplement, an energy drink or an app to monitor it all, as Mick told me, 'there is always an innovative solution for everything'.

More than ever before, people are looking to technology and innovations to solve their problems. In the past, a person like Mick might have realised that he was staying up too late or that perhaps all those stimulants during the day were keeping him awake at night, but not now. Mick is part of the first generation to grow up in the digital world, and he turns to the marketplace for his solutions. He and many like him want a quick fix to their problems and view innovation and technology as the go-to for product excellence. Of course, these amazing designs have also helped to create and foster a new society of super-impatient consumers.

However, without knowledge of these new psychological and sociological shifts, retailers are relying on simple historical sales data and marketing tactics, even as we know they aren't working as they once did. And it's no wonder they're not working – our consumers have changed all around us and we are still working off marketing and retailing strategies that focused on consumers long gone.

New studies are being published daily, and experts are finding more and more associations with technology – good and bad. Please don't think I'm a technophobe – I'm definitely not. I absolutely adore it. But every research corridor I went down led to more and more information on how and why consumers were changing due to technology.

It's also important to mention that while I have been cautious with the harvesting of world-class information and studies included here, by necessity we use data from the past to predict the future. With such massive changes being recorded, it simply begs the question: if we use our 'past data' to predict the 'future', how relevant will it actually be? Now, more than ever, it is a risk for retailers to assume the future is a continuation of the past.

Now, this may seem like a bit of pandemonium, but some aspects are clear. Customers are buying to satiate their heightened emotional states and to fix their problems, and are increasingly relying on technology and new innovations to do so. Knowing this, don't you want to know how and where you can help them? Wouldn't it be handy to know what motivates this new customer to shop with you regularly and to become interested in what you offer and have to say? I believe so, which is why I researched this topic for years, performed an experiment in my very own store and then decided to write a book on it all. So let's continue with our understanding of the changes in consumers so we can then focus on what we can do to combat them in-store.

ISOLATION AND OUR NEED FOR HUMAN CONNECTION

Scientists have long thought our large brains and ability for abstract thought and planning is what made the human species such a success story. But it wasn't just our big brain that helped us outfox our enemies. Neuroscience has recently discovered it was actually our ability to create large, collaborative networks, and form lasting relationships.

Deep human connection is our strongest motivator to succeed, learn and grow. The larger front part of the brain, our prefrontal cortex, combined with our ability to understand another human's state of mind was critical to us in those early days of forming connections. Indeed, our need to belong and connect is rooted in our very survival. In the caveman times, if you were not part of a community, you and your genes did not survive. So, in a way, everyone who is alive today has stemmed from those who learned to connect to fight, procure food and belong to a group or community.[12]

> To improve is to change; to be perfect is to change often.
>
> *Winston Churchill*

Our need to have meaningful human connection is right up there with our need for food, water and shelter. While scientists attribute human connection as being the foundation of happiness and the source of our meaning in life, we now find ourselves in a new era where the human race is becoming increasingly alone and extremely isolated.

So although we are predisposed to connection, we awkwardly find ourselves in the position of surviving alone. We are disconnecting from the very social fabric known to our genes and opting for a seemingly less anxious, less time-consuming and less interdependent social connection than ever before.

Increased isolation has been led by several shifts in society today. First off, families are no longer staying or living near each other as they once did. Secondly, our increased use of technology and social media leads to further isolation. As outlined by Gartner,

Nearly 60 per cent of social network users say they feel more connected to people now than they did previously. In the same exact survey, 55 per cent of them also said they have less face-to-face contact with friends, and 32 per cent said they feel lonelier now than they did previously.[13]

Digital communication can be meaningful, but it's less intimate than face-to-face contact and, generally speaking, what we share through technology is usually more superficial in nature.

Now you may be wondering, *What the hell does isolation have to do with retailing?* Well, as I noted at the beginning of the chapter, understanding people and how they are feeling is imperative to our retail messaging and our store environments.

It seems one thing is sure: the less we interact with each other as a species, the more self-focused we become. This drives further isolation, resulting in less face-to-face time with friends and loved ones. Here are some more recent statistics in this area:

- Loneliness has doubled to 40 per cent of adults in two recent surveys, up from 20 per cent in the 1980s.[14]

- In Australia in 1975, 16 per cent of people lived alone before marriage. Skip ahead to 2013, and over 77 per cent live alone before marriage.[15]

- In an experiment conducted in 2013, people who felt isolated or excluded made riskier financial decisions and had a greater appetite for gambling.[16]

Now, as you can see, this vicious circle is not only happening in the real world with families, colleagues and individuals, but also exists in our retail world as well. As our customers withdraw from anxious situations – including pushy salespeople and oversized stores with too much choice – they begin purchasing more and more online, and become even more self-focused on satisfying their needs and wants through retailers. As we underwhelm customers on their store visits, we push them further and further away.

From our side of the situation, as retailers, we see fewer customers in-store and, in turn, we also begin focusing more and more inwardly, not on what the customer needs but what we need more of – sales. We notice that online sales erode our profit and get angry – not just with the customers but also with our own digital and e-commerce departments. Neither the retailer nor the customer is satisfied, yet neither seems ready to change; it's a Mexican standoff.

On the other hand, though, there has never been a better time in history for retailers to stand up, show their true personality and connect with their customers in a meaningful way – especially because not many are doing this. Because of this sense of isolation and the intense emotions in play, people are more prone now than ever to adore a retailer if they just reach out and connect and give back some value. Later in the book, I talk about specific strategies that help to connect and bring that human touch into your four walls of retail.

THE RISE IN DISTRUST, THE RISE IN INDIVIDUALISM

I've been following the Edelman Trust Barometer since about 2012; however, it's been recording and gathering statistics from over 33,000 respondents in 28 countries since 2000. With more than 17 years under its belt now, the Trust Barometer is a good indicator of people's trust in government, business, media and other people in general. Over the last few years in particular, it has been steadily tracking the rise of distrust in government.

In 2016, for example, they found about half of the surveyed countries were 'distrusters'; however, the 2017 results are in and this has risen to over two-thirds of countries defined as distrusters.[17] While trust in government has taken a huge hit, Edelman's report outlines the opportunities for business to step up in these uncertain political times. As reported, trust in business remains higher than that for government or media. However, this doesn't mean business or retailers are out of the woods completely.

Perhaps most concerning for business is the connection between the public's fears and business's role in worsening them. Of the respondents, 60 per cent had worries about losing their job to globalisation and foreign competition. So while Amazon is a real fear and noteworthy opponent, retailers have a distinct advantage if they can communicate their value proposition and humanise their brand locally with customers.

Remaining locally relevant

So what's the power in local? Some of the most successful retailers and businesses have been using locally relevant strategies for years. Starbucks, for instance, while being a huge company, has based its success on remaining locally relevant wherever it opens up shop. Even internationally, its expansion plans into India differed considerably from those in China, US or its European stores. For instance, in their expansion plans in China, Starbucks have partnered with Tmall, which allows gifting options for its digitally trendy Chinese customers. Starbucks did this to showcase their digital innovations to the market. Starbucks will also focus on their 'reserve' stores in China, which are highly specialised experience stores, with rare and exquisite coffee only available in limited quantities globally. Starbucks' approach in India, on the other hand, acknowledged this was predominately a tea-drinking nation. The company's launch of Teavana in the country will help Starbucks gain customers in the region.

Starbucks have always done this – whether their focus is on an international approach or a national approach inside their origins in the US. Starbucks has remained true to its purpose in being the local community hub.

What I'm getting at here is that your retail store must continue to be *locally relevant*, regardless of whether it's part of a big national chain. Indeed, huge conglomerates have known this to be true for years, and are well known for buying up small startups to appear smaller, or making local adaptation as already outlined.

Consumers would rather buy from a more localised retailer; the only thing holding them back is that these retailers usually don't have the bells and whistles that the nationalised big chains do.

Inevitably, when polled, consumers go back to the bigger chain stores for convenience, for the price, for range and the newest trends and technologies. But what if you could provide those very comforting things as a franchisor, corporate or large buying group while still being the preferred local retailer in your community? Well, it's the best of both worlds for the customer.

Becoming more human

For me, the formula for increased distrust from consumers looks like this:

> **1 part de-humanising + 1 part consumer empowerment = consumer distrust**

This means, when we know one of our symptoms for what's wrong in retailing is distrust, a great remedy for this distrust is humanising. Getting involved with your local customers and showing off your personality will help personify your business. Later in the book, I have the whole of part IV devoted to humanising your retail store. For now, just recognise that growing distrust stems from not being transparent and hiding behind false corporate missions and mumbo-jumbo. People love to buy and shop with other real people and what they stand for – not soulless brands.

The second part of distrust comes from the social changes in individualism or what many refer to as 'consumer empowerment'. While consumers may trust business more than they do government or media, that trust is still low. Meaning, retailers need to understand several strategies when dealing with empowered consumers.

New York Times columnist David Brooks recently discussed Google's database of 5.2 million books published between 1500 and 2008. He notes a sharp increase in the words and phrases like 'self', 'I come first', 'personalised', along with a sharp decrease in communal words like 'common good', 'community' and 'collective'. Brooks summarised his finding by saying,

> Over the past half-century, society has become more
> individualistic. As it has become more individualistic,
> it has also become less morally aware, because social
> and moral fabrics are inextricably linked.[18]

Online recommendations are now the bedrock of all e-commerce sites; it's no surprise that consumers like and trust what other purchasers say about a product. This links in with the latest findings from the Edelman's Trust Barometer. According to the 2017 findings from Edelman,[19] the top spokespeople who were deemed as extremely or very credible, in order of importance, were the following:

- a technical expert (preferred by 67 per cent of respondents)

- an academic expert (65 per cent)

- 'a person like you' (63 per cent).

At the lowest end of the scale, and much further down the list, were government officials at 35 per cent of respondents! Yikes, tough crowd. Also note that just a bit further down from 'a person like you' came employees of your business, sitting at around 50 per cent.

So consumers now see 'a person like you', or someone who they connect with as having similar values and needs, as suddenly a very credible source. Of course, this is ideal for digital because this source can be easily curated through online recommendations and served up on a real-time scenario on your website.

However, for retailers, this distrust statistic reveals a further gap in our in-store environments. Business employees weighing in at a mere 50 per cent on the credibility scale highlights that using real-life experts can seriously enhance your in-store offering. Offering a specialised ambience and serving up a simplified list of choices, experts and academics can work for retailers to create a sense of local community and trusted expertise right within your own store.

So there you have it, our new empowered consumer trusts strangers who've posted recommendations online, only slightly below technical and academic experts. Go figure?

So if we review the earlier equation on the rise of distrust as:

1 part de-humanising + 1 part consumer empowerment = consumer distrust

And then re-arrange it based on what we've just learned, it might look something like this:

Humanise your store + credible experts in-store = building trust

NARCISSISM IN RETAIL

Most of our customers today express some degree of self-focus and superficiality (mild narcissism). Retailers and retail marketers must understand what drives this narcissism to better understand customers.

As with most things, narcissism can range from healthy to downright clinically destructive. On one side, it is a desire to better yourself and grow, shown in a self-interest to improve, but not at the expense of others. On the other end of the spectrum, it looks a bit scarier – with an explosion of self-importance, complete lack of empathy for others, need for admiration and extreme sensitivity to criticism. Hmm, sound like someone you know? As Jeremy Dean notes,

Twitter is often uncharitably said to be perfect for our narcissistic age. It enables people to gather followers, talk about themselves, all without having to listen to anyone else.[20]

From a purchasing standpoint, emotions and narcissism are intrinsically linked. For us retailers, understanding narcissism means that you better understand what your customers need from you.

Tap into your inner-psychologist

It is with this focus on us, the human, the decision-maker, the narcissist and the purchaser that I dedicate this little rant. Regardless of your fancy-dancy marketing and retailing techniques, without an accurate understanding of what is happening both psychologically and physically to our fellow human beings, how can we truly understand what our customers want and need from us as retailers? Without this understanding, we will never be privy to the real changes that are happening right within our own stores and how we can fix emerging problems.

Putting everything that happens in your store down to marketing is too easy. True, when retail marketing really works, it seems almost magical. To those who aren't marketers, what can be produced may appear as a sacred gift only a few mortals possess. However, it couldn't be further from the truth or more harmful for retail owners and managers to think that way. These fallacies keep you from thinking and actively observing customers' reactions. In short, they distance you from where you need to be – right smack dab in the thick of it, getting to know what drives and makes your own customer tick.

Now, I know you can't spend all your time with customers – you have a retail empire to attend to, after all – but make sure at least once or twice a week you allocate 30 minutes to connecting with customers and walking around in your store(s). Talk to them, serve them and find out what makes them tick, what they like and what they don't like.

On the flipside however, when marketing fails, fewer customers come through the door, and you start to hear statements like, 'That idea has been done to death', or people blame how busy the marketplace is, saying something like, 'You'll need to stand out to be different'. The simple revelation is that when marketing is effective, the same ideas work repeatedly because they resonate deeply within us – in our minds and emotionally within our hearts. There is nothing magical about it; the magic is only in knowing why and how we shop and buy things, and recognising a change in customer behaviour and acting accordingly. Importantly, retailers need to focus less on features and benefits of a product and a lot more on the emotional and social factors. (I provide more on this topic in part IV.)

Out of pure curiosity, I decided to not leave it up to the marketing 'experts', and I started researching and studying how and why our customers were changing and, of course, what I could do to turn them around and get them re-engaged with us.

I know a lot of retailers and behind every great one is a closet psychologist who somehow, even accidentally, deeply understands humans. In fact, you may not officially recognise this as a skill set in yourself, but you innately know that people purchase and buy for more than just necessity. Not just because neuroscience has proved the dopamine rush of a good retail therapy session, but because you have a good handle on what makes people tick. Usually these same closet psychologists, you know the ones, are good at sales too. As a really good retailer, you might even understand how the human mind works and identify with the different personalities, egos and emotions that come into play.

Many philosophers have attributed the art of persuasion to man's ability to understand the human emotions. In fact, Aristotle elaborated on this, arguing that one essential part of persuading an audience was to 'understand the emotions – that is, to name them and describe them, to know their causes and the way in which they are excited' and that the 'persuasion may come through the hearers, when the speech stirs their emotions'.

Retailers with this deep understanding of emotion are the quickest to recognise and understand changes are needed in our industry. These retailers identify customers' needs and changes, and also own up that we, as retailers, aren't really helping our customers to be drawn to us – instead, we are pushing them away. Largely, we are self-serving and in love with our products and not our customers, and this is what I hope to help shine a light on in this book.

A bit on retail marketing return on investment

Nokia's CEO Steve Ballmer ended his parting speech by saying, 'We didn't do anything wrong but, somehow, we lost'. Several years ago, retailers went about marketing budgets in a fairly methodical way. We allocated a percentage of our marketing into branding and into price and product through TV, press, digital, some partnerships and store giveaways. We scheduled regular sale-day campaigns, catalogues and watched the people arrive in-store to buy our excellent 'merchandise'.

Like me, you've probably also noticed that in the last seven years, fewer and fewer people are responding to these traditional campaigns. So what do we do as retailers? We collect a bit more money from our suppliers and create even more clever campaigns, spend more and more to get fewer people through the door.

This continuous decline of the return on investment (ROI) in marketing is at the very heart of why the new customer I have outlined through this chapter is so important. If we don't understand the *why*, we not only won't shift our focus but also won't understand the underlying reasoning to do so or the messaging that will resonate.

As a retail owner, franchisee, manager or otherwise, you don't need to be an expert in consumer psychology, but you do need to understand, take note and shift focus on this new customer.

I love retail and retailers and I don't want anyone to have to close their doors with the same bewildered look on their face as Nokia's Steve Ballmer – wondering why they somehow lost.

CONNECTING THE NEW CUSTOMERS WITH RETAILERS

So we know that our customers have changed and that you and I have changed significantly due to technology and isolation and just plain ol' being busy. People are anxious and stressed and have less time. So, retailers who curate experiences and products are helping customers more than those who simply try to sell more 'stuff'. Helpful retailers will be emphasising the importance of customer relationships first, and then using technology and online offers and support to aid in their effectiveness.

We also know that our customers are more isolated than ever before, and are scanning for retailers who are like them. Retailers who are tapping into their own customers' preferences and insights and really helping them in fresh new ways – these are the retailers who are trusted, rewarded with loyalty and even talked about with family and friends.

Neuroscience has proven that engaging consumers is not so much about social selling or consumer groups and accessing whether they are 'early adopters' or 'laggards'; it's actually more deeply rooted than that. It's about being totally empathetic to your customers and understanding their emotional needs too.

At the heart of it all, what I recognised after a year or so of researching consumer psychology and customer experience is that our focus shouldn't be on finding more efficient ways to sell more stuff, increase profit or retailing space. I realised I really needed to adjust my retailing mindset and, for once, consider that maybe I had it wrong. Maybe, just maybe, if I stopped chasing and pushing and selling, and instead started focusing on serving, empathising and giving back, the laws of reciprocity would finally be on my side. And you know what? It worked.

CHA
SHOF
ENVIRONN

2

While stores themselves have been greatly affected by changes around them, the *context* of our retail stores have remained unchanged for over 200 years. Sure, we've added some new things like beacons, video displays or a 'Silent Salesman', and some have invested in more technology and solutions like augmented or virtual reality, but by and large most of our stores haven't changed all that much from what they used to be.

Yet our in-store environments are quite a bit different, aren't they? Just five years ago most retailers, regardless of their product line, would have had more customers in-store, and so they'd have had a different sort of ambiance happening. In addition, most would have had more staff around the place too.

The terrible thing about the internet and Amazon is that they take the magic and happy chaos out of book shopping. The internet might give you what you want, but it won't give you what you need.

Tom Hodgkinson

So while we haven't made that many physical changes to the inside of our retail stores, it's fair to say that stores have changed quite significantly in other ways.

Over the past several years, I've uncovered five major issues that are deeply affecting our in-store environments today:

1   *Retailers are distracted by online sales, technology and data:* While technology is supposed to make our lives easier, it has complicated and distanced our relationships with the end customer.

2   *Consumer expectations have changed:* Today, retailers are not evaluated on their competitors but on the global experiences their customers have everywhere. It's a tall order, but customers now have a whole different set of expectations in-store.

3   *The volume of browsing has declined:* Overall, fewer people are browsing and, with fewer people in-store, the environment becomes less exciting. When you see a shop full of people – like the Apple store, for example – you want to see what you're missing.

4   *Physical stores' roles have changed significantly:* Bricks-and-mortar stores represent a different role to consumers now, especially as the way people get information has changed. Just several years ago, the majority of people still spoke to salespeople for their product knowledge. Now, over 87 per cent do their research before stepping foot in a store.

5   *Shopping behaviours and habits have shifted:* We are more time-poor, isolated and anxious and have less interest in 'things' than ever before.

The following sections look at these five areas in more detail.

ELEPHANT IN THE ROOM: ONLINE SALES

You'll notice I don't really talk a lot about online shopping. I'm not avoiding the topic and I don't feel negatively about it in any way. It's the opposite, actually; I see online shopping as an absolute necessity and also a natural progression of retail due to our busy lives, the technology available and psychological shifts in society today.

Online retail is super-important to your business because some people just don't have the time to shop in-store, or don't want to shop or be around people. Others feel real anxiety about shopping, while others randomly happen to see your Google advert or find your adverts on social media and impulse-buy something they've been meaning to get in-store for weeks. And, for many products, seeing them beforehand or buying them in person is completely unnecessary.

If you have a whole store of 'things' that people don't need to see or buy in person, though, you will be fighting a constant uphill battle. Unless you control production and distribution, you'll be competing mainly on price and today, with the likes of Amazon and others, that's not a race I'd be willing to run.

Either way, keeping your eye on the digital ball is an absolute necessity, especially given that the majority of bricks-and-mortar purchases are either started or finished online. A whole universe of totally awesome online 'peeps' is out there to help you with all that jazz, but I'm not one of them. As Austin Powers once said, 'It's not my bag, baby.'

In fact, this is about the only section where online is even addressed in this book, and that's because it does directly affect the area that is near and dear to my heart: the in-store environment. The proliferation of online shopping and searching has deeply affected in-store sales and shopping in general. Let's look at some of the detail on why.

Crunching the online numbers

Today, out of $100 spent in Australian retail, only $6.34 will be spent online. If we go back to just six years ago, it's much smaller again, to being barely even negligible. My point is that the vast majority – in fact, $317 billion to be precise – of overall spend is spent in retail, with only $20.1 billion spent online.[1] So while we have had years of huge online growth, spent endless hours in boardrooms discussing new tech, infrastructure and online strategies, we also should recognise where the majority of our focus should be, right? Or do we?

Retailers and certainly our marketing teams spend a lot of time focusing on an income stream that produces anywhere from 1 to 7 per cent of our total sales and represents even less in profit. Don't get me wrong; as I said, I know online is absolutely important. If you don't focus on this area and have a great digital team, that percentage will surely go to your competitor. And, of course, online will continue to grow, meaning that figure will blow out.

The online world isn't just about sales, however. In 2014, Google released findings from its study on the digital impact on in-store shopping,[2] highlighting that 87 per cent of consumers seek information about a product before even stepping into a store. Google's findings also showed that 79 per cent of people continue this search for information while in-store and 35 per cent of customers still seek further information after purchase. The majority of the search for information before and after purchase is conducted online, but customers are also resorting to online research while in-store, with Google finding 71 per cent of in-store shoppers who use smartphones for online research say their device has become more important to their in-store experience. Clearly, this trend of using technology to aid in decision-making is here to stay.

... But, what if?

Let's shift focus a little and look at your reports for a minute – say, yesterday's figures. If you're anything like me, the first thing you do every morning is look at your figures from yesterday, checking aspects like your visitation rate, sales, profit and product mixes compared to same time last year, last week and last month.

In my previous business, we had a 'What if?' report. It was based on the fact that you could run the 'What if?' report by switching your focus on a particular retail metric. For example, 'What if you increased your warranties or sales by x per cent?' or 'What if you sold more products in a particular category that had a higher gross profit?' It was a nice little trick, and I often used it to play out scenarios with the staff, managers and myself. Running the report wasn't just about increasing that metric – if that were the case, you could simply add 2 per cent onto your sales figures yourself. No, the report actually looked at that figure and then projected how the increase would affect your profit, stock rotations and estimated rebates, and you could look at that scenario for a week, month or year.

I bring this up because, as you know, retail is all about focusing on particular areas and then seeing how that plays out over the long term. Sure, 1 per cent sounds like child's play, but if you can sustain this over a longer period, even an increase as small as this can have a huge financial impact on what you make, what the organisation makes, how many staff you can keep on and so on.

So my question to you – even though I've taken a roundabout way of getting there – is this: what if you increased focus on in-store customers and brought your in-store sales and visitation up by just 1 per cent, day on day? With that in mind, now think about how that 1 per cent might affect your sales, profit, impulse purchases, warranty or other add-on sales and stock rotation.

And how would those extra people in-store affect the vibe of your staff, other customers and salespeople? Do you think those extra people might also have an impact on how other customers visiting the store think about where they are at? Of course it would. How do you feel when you are in an Apple Store? I always feel like something is going to happen and I'll miss out on it if I leave.

Yes, technology and the online experience are here to stay, but can you keep your eye on the ball with digital while also turning your in-store experience up a notch? Sure you can; it's all about focus, and that is precisely what this book is all about.

For now, we can start by simply recognising that digital is extremely important to our businesses. Most of us have gurus to drive this and keep it up, however, so let's leave them to it. Secondly, let's admit we've dropped another ball because of our tech and digital obsession. By focusing back on our in-store environments and the in-person customer, even a small increase in our efforts could make a massive change to our trading environment, our customers, our staff, sales and profitability, and stock turns.

So while technology is supposed to make all of our lives easier (hello, the 1.5 hours I lost on Facebook earlier today!), it can also make us lose sight of the bigger picture and bigger percentage of our business. Sure, the tech and analytics is fun but, especially as retailers, our bread and butter – saleswise and influence-wise – is in-store.

Retail, technology and data

As already mentioned, many physical retail adaptations have been made as of late. However, these seem to have been developed not really in response to consumers' needs but based on what the retail technology industry can manufacture and sell to the retailers as the next best thing.

Sure, my observation here is a bit tongue in cheek. Many new tech developments are initially based on a particular retailer's legitimate customer. However, no tech can come close to the often messy, expensive and somewhat downplayed human connection. If done right, a human connection will always 'trump' any type of technology.

My point is, tech solutions have many times been developed and then later scaled for profit. After all, researching, designing and building new technology isn't cheap, so this technology is then on-sold to retailers as the next best thing for their success. Really, though, it was meant to serve a particular market or need, which is simply not shared by all retailers.

All this chasing to find the next big thing that will woo our customers has left many traditional bricks-and-mortar stores looking at their competitors instead of their very own customers for answers.

Our real relationship with customers

I delve more deeply into the importance of building relationships with customers later in the book, but the topic deserves a quick mention while we're discussing the changes to our in-store environment. People-to-people connections are the strongest and most memorable of all connections. We connect more deeply when connecting in-person. People are able to understand nonverbal cues and have more empathy for humans than even the most 'human-like' tech that we have today. Because we are human ourselves, we simply understand other people better than machines do.

When your customer service staff asks someone how they found their shopping experience on a particular day and that person scrunches up their nose and tilts their head while saying, 'It was pretty good', you pretty much know you didn't cut the mustard with that customer. But, by empathising with them and digging deeper on what you could do then and there to help them, this says you care. Ask them in a survey, and they'd probably tick the 'okay' box.

Relying solely on analytics and data may seem like the most scientific and fool-proof method. Trust me; I'm a scientist at heart – I studied genetics and biology and even worked in a lab for some time. I'm highly analytic and love a scientific approach. However, as I touched on in chapter 1, people don't always do what they say they will do in a survey. When emotions come into play in purchasing and evaluating, we often don't act or react the way our rational mind says we will.

Formulating bonds is best left to people and if 'your people' are only shopping online with you, re-engaging them and truly helping them with solving their problems is hard and costly.

CONSUMER EXPECTATIONS HAVE CHANGED

As covered earlier in this chapter, 87 per cent of our customers today seek out information before even entering our stores – researching the rational details like features, comparing different brands and recommendations, and confirming styles, colours, stock and pricing online. Assuming you've satiated these rational choices with customers online before they come to your store, your salespeople are then left with little room to woo these customers with extreme product knowledge in-store. In fact, many customers – and especially those under 25 – already have the information they need when they arrive in-store, so their expectations are entirely different.

With globalisation and digital playing huge parts in all of our lives, our experiences on Instagram or Pinterest influence our expectations in physical spaces too. Just as decorating our homes is now influenced by catwalk fashion, so too are the expectations of customers who visit our showrooms – we've all grown accustomed to looking at beautiful vignettes, colour-themed products and brightly coloured food posts. ('Vignettes' is an interior design term for merchandising.)

Merchandising that stages and features the ingredients and products for a fun dinner party with friends is emotive, fun, and exciting – and it makes us want to host a dinner party ourselves. Taking customers on a journey with an expert – who can give them home styling tips for a cocktail party of their own, for example, or teach them how to prepare and cook a dinner party that everyone will post on Instagram – can also have the same effect.

The point is, expectations have changed, and retailers who look at these lifestyle trends, colours and emotions as passages to endear their customers and fulfil their deepest desires of fitting in, having fun and connecting with friends and family in new, fresh ways are the ones customers are listening to as advisors.

Currently most customers don't consciously expect an emotional experience in-store, but I think in the very near future this will be the primary driver of sales in bricks-and-mortar stores. You must genuinely know what your customers want emotionally and deliver on that promise in a very real and visceral way.

Leave the product statistics and the features online and bring the emotions, inspiration and education into your showroom and you will soon find what deeply resonates with your best customers.

VOLUME OF BROWSING HAS DECLINED

When I was at university in Chicago, we had a variety of parties we could attend on the weekends – and let's just say I've always been the social sort. As the week came to an end, various flyers and pieces of information would be passed around campus. Some parties I'd hear about through friends in my sorority or through classmates, and sometimes we'd hear things from the local watering hole on the corner. Whatever the source, we always had abundant choices for where to go each weekend.

With all this choice, sometimes you'd have to check out the place before you committed. And so I'd set out with my homies to find the best on offer. The majority of the time, the first place we'd visit would be fairly empty, simply because it was still pretty early and not that many people were out yet. But one place – Danny's – always had a big crowd, even if it was early. We'd walk in to find heaps of people and, more times than not, if he was having a party, we'd end up staying there.

I was commenting at school one day about how his place was always packed and he said, 'Yeah, of course it is. I make sure a musician is scheduled earlier in the day.' In a very confidential discussion, he shared with me that he paid his entire month's rent just with the proceeds of his once a month keg party. I often wondered if this was true because rent in Chicago was pretty pricey and his place was modern, big and in the perfect location. 'Yup', he responded, before elaborating: 'The most important part is getting a good musician so that people stick around for when the later crowd comes by.' He went on to explain that he didn't charge during the day, but the night-time crowd was where the money was. He was well aware of the 'walk-by' crowd and purposely held something earlier that was mostly free so that the paying party goers would see the crowd and stay at his place. Very clever indeed.

Many other people running those parties had super-cool flyers highlighting which DJs were playing, but if we showed up and things didn't seem that exciting, we still moved on to the next place.

I'd love to know what Danny's up to these days because he was quite the entrepreneur at nineteen, but I do know this: he knew his customers, and he knew the importance of a good crowd and experience.

As we lose customers online or to other competitors, our stores have fewer and fewer people visiting. As we fight the uphill battle of customers moving on, like those parties back in my university days, we start struggling to attract anyone. Regardless of whether you have the best copy on your website or branding, if you've got no-one visiting your store, you'll have very big and real problems connecting with the people paying your bills – your customers.

As retailers, we must appreciate and understand the considerable importance of developing new and innovative ways to get customers into our stores. It's imperative that we don't throw our hands up in the air and concede to the beautiful and shiny growth of online sales – even if it's our own growth. Without the hustle and bustle of people inside our beautiful stores, they become a lot less interesting for everyone.

So don't wait till it's too late, do something now. Stop right now and think about Danny's party. At what times during the day do you see an increase in visitation into your store? How can you make sure you already have a good number of people there for when they arrive? Can you purposely offer something valuable and *free* to ensure you've always got something fun happening for when the shoppers come in? Make sure you write down your thoughts and capture some ideas.

PHYSICAL STORES' ROLES HAVE CHANGED SIGNIFICANTLY

In their heyday, large department stores were a mecca for theatre, intrigue and fun. Department stores would decorate their windows and foreshadow the most exciting products and trends. Passersby would window-shop with envy, and in-store shoppers would enjoy the magic with their entire family. Then, new end-cap displays and products would proudly show off things customers had never seen before.

Here's how *Ackermann's Repository* (an illustrated British periodical published from 1809–1829) explains in around 1811 one of the first of these types of retailers, for example:

> It is fitted up with great taste, and divided by glazed partitions into four departments. These were: furs and fans; haberdashery of every description, silks, muslins, lace, gloves etc.; jewellery and ornamental items including perfumery; and finally, millinery and dresses; so that there is no article of female attire or decoration, but what may be here procured in the first style of elegance and fashion.

Today, however, new trends are posted directly on social media or sent to our inbox well before we step foot in a retail store. So how do we surprise and delight these new clued-up and cynical customers who have seen it all – last week? How do we razzle and dazzle them like the olden days but with a new twist?

Here is where I'm a huge fan of technology – when it's used to make the customers' experience extraordinary, and used as a tool to heighten their senses and their overall experience in your store.

I recently attended a retail conference where staff from retailer Neiman Marcus talked about their 'Magic Mirrors' and 'Beauty

Makeover Mirrors'. These mirrors have built-in cameras and social sharing tools, so as a customer you can try on your favourite outfit and send it straight to a friend for advice. You can also take short videos of you in the outfit (as you turn around, for example). The make-up makeover mirror provides customers with their very own educational video and tutorial of how a make-up artist would apply the products, sharing their techniques and product details like the colour and brand that was used during the makeover. All of this is sent with links to your smartphone for either social sharing or just to review when you get home.

Too many stores, however, are way behind on this type of thinking. My friend Kimberly, for example, once told me of her retail debacle. She lived quite a distance from me and was interested in a new and expensive ($800) blender. Like many others, she had done her research online – in fact, she told me she'd done over three hours of research all up.

After all this research, Kimberly was keen to buy a particular blender but wanted to visit a retail store first. She shared with me that she wanted to hear what the staff had to say about it, wanted to touch the product and get a feel for why these bloody new blenders were so expensive when her last one was $69. Was it worth it? What does the handle feel like, and will it be heavy on her wrist (injured a few years back)? So she started her physical journey.

Sure, fewer people like Kimberly are arriving in-store to browse. Some won't even make it to the store and will be comfortable with purchasing the blender online. But others still want to feel it, touch it and get some feedback from another human rather than relying on online recommendations – after all, it's a big purchase. However, when Kimberly finally arrived in the store, her first impressions weren't great – the store was so empty she wondered if they were even open. And then, the experience only got worse.

After her three hours of research, Kimberly felt she could have sold the blender to anyone in that store, and it was obvious to her that the person assisting her didn't know as much as she did about it. By now, she felt like she'd just wasted her time.

That's when she decided to call me, her friend who owned a store that sold these fancy-dancy blenders. She didn't want to 'bother' me but wanted to ask me some questions. Her reservations were mainly about wanting to make nut butters and some very specific things with this blender, and not being sure it was right for the job. Lucky for me, I have the same blender and know all about it, so I could tell her what she needed to know and she bought one … finally. All up, this was a four-month process for Kimberly.

This sort of experience plays out in-store everywhere. What generally happens is that consumers get conditioned in-store to feel like the retailer has just wasted their time. They know more about the features and benefits of the product, its price and how it's used than the people working in the store selling the things. Of course, after this kind of experience the next time they think about purchasing they may elect to just buy online – or change it up altogether and buy from a competitor.

One thing is very clear: customers are becoming more and more disengaged with retailers as we under-deliver and provide less and less value to them. It's a catch 22: as retailers themselves further encourage online purchasing, consumers realise it's easier and more convenient (and less frustrating) to buy that way. The trade-off is that now consumers don't know or care *who* they buy from – their decision is mainly based on price and trust of the e-tailer.

This vicious circle continues round and round – as customers feel like they're wasting their time in-store, in exchange they stick it to the retailer by going online. This 'tit for tat' is, in essence, worth more than their own time. It's clear that while Kimberly was expecting far greater things in-store, she left feeling disappointed.

We'd do well as retailers to remember a famous quote from Steve Jobs – just replace the

> You've got to start with the customer experience and work backwards to the technology. A lot of times people don't know what they want until you show it to them.
>
> *Steve Jobs*

word 'technology' in the quote with the word 'retailing' and it sums the situation up nicely for our industry.

As a side note to Kimberly's story, when we developed our first ever Paleo show at a retailer that was close to where my friend Kimberly lived (more on these events later), I invited her along. The event included an in-depth look at making nut butters and cashew cheese and was facilitated by a well-known Paleo expert – Leah, who had had an autoimmune disease years prior. Leah was extremely passionate about health and diet and was on a mission to show those with autoimmune and other chronic health issues that manufactured food was a major contributor.

Kimberly recently purchased her $800 blender and was gob-smacked by all the information Leah presented her with. She told me this kind of information was exactly what she had been look-ing for. When I asked her if attending an educational workshop like this would have helped her back in her buying phase she said, 'Absolutely. I probably would have bought something that day, not four months later.' She didn't know what she wanted before the event, but she loved the advice and insight that our Paleo expert provided – and was incredibly grateful to her local retailer for pro-viding this insight for *free*.

What are the 'hang-ups' your customers have? What keeps them from making a purchasing decision on something they think they want? What blows out that decision-making process from days into months? What are some of the issues your customers face or have trouble with? These could be issues involving saving time, saving money or avoiding pain.

In the example of Kimberly, while she was interested in a prod-uct – the blender – she was *more* interested in the lifestyle benefits, tips and learnings of how to adopt this new journey of making her food from scratch rather than relying on the food manufacturing industry.

And as a final part of the story, I'm happy to report that Kim-berly is now a converted Paleo person. She uses her blender a lot and posts a gazillion pictures on Instagram of her creations. She's lost about 15 kilograms and feels great. It's so much nicer helping people rather than just 'selling' them stuff, don't you think?

SHOPPING BEHAVIOURS AND HABITS HAVE SHIFTED

In chapter 1 we looked at the new customer. Part of this is a progression away from people simply wanting more 'things' to craving more experiences and transformations – an idea explored in great detail in *The Experience Economy* by B Joseph Pine II and James H Gilmore, originally published in 1999. Well and truly before their time, Pine and Gilmore argue that businesses should come up with memorable events for their customers, and that the memory itself will then become the product – the 'experience' is the focus, rather than the commoditised product you are selling. As this trend continues, I don't think people will stop wanting things altogether, and so stop shopping. Instead, this trend signifies a definite shift in what people are looking for and what shopping needs to deliver to customers while in-store.

In Roy Morgan Research's *State of the Nation Retail Spotlight* report, CEO Michele Levine says,

The fact that Australians are spending more on 'experiences' (leisure activities outside the home) and less on 'things' (discretionary commodities) is one the most striking findings … Of course, this doesn't mean retail is dead: just that it needs to adapt to this growing desire for experiences and entertainment.[3]

In fact, many times, I've found that my clients' products – or 'things' – may just be the very tools they need for the transformations and experiences their customers are seeking.

Our Instagram and Facebook feeds may be full of fun, wacky selfies on the weekend, specialty cocktails with friends and hiking pics with the family – all while the feeds we see from retailers are filled with 'things'. The latest sunglasses or handbag; a new dining room set or a car. Zzzzzz, can anyone say boring?

Imagine now that you could have customers in your store taking photos of your 'things' while having fun or being silly. Imagine they are in your store learning from or being inspired by someone who also thinks your stuff is pretty cool – in fact, these experts use your products and work within an industry that means they can speak quite intelligently about the pros and cons, and about the ins and outs of getting into this type of 'thing'. Let go of everything and anything that is perfect and let people have 100 per cent real experiences – this is a true, no-holds-barred retail experience.

Forethought into what your customers do in their downtime and what interesting trends are emerging, and how you can bring these things to life inside your store is what will get customers sharing and experiencing why your store is different.

Forget about the retail haters and the doom and gloom prophecies of how Amazon will destroy your business. Instead, embrace *how* your store can excite more people to have fun, be inspired and to take photos in-store. Create a space for your customers that's all about them, that's worth a selfie, that inspires an entertaining story to share at dinner. After all, isn't that the real-life version of what a net promoter score is all about?

RETAILERS ... THE SAME, ONLY DIFFERENT

When you look at the retail industry overall, it's not only vastly different but also has some crazy similarities. Our differences are in the people we all serve. A camping retailer and a luxury fashion retailer, for example, might have different experiences for their customers, but they both have stores, both face global pressure and are both in need of engaging their customers.

So, while our customers may vary dramatically, what doesn't differ is that just like you, we all have a physical retail platform. Regardless of the products you sell, you need your customers to listen and be engaged, and they need to trust you.

It's time to start reimagining your retail space and what it can be used for. Time to start thinking of not just delivering products but also delivering experiences, learning and inspiration.

While the fit-out and design of our stores may have changed, and definitely the ratio of customers to staff has changed, the idea of walking into a store, looking for something you like, paying for it and taking it with you is remarkably unchanged.

As we draw closer to 2020, over 200 years since the opening of the first department stores, we find ourselves in a dramatically different retail landscape. As already covered in this chapter, changes in globalisation, social and family structures and technology have threatened what it means to be a retailer today. But your key to thriving and adapting lies right inside your store every day.

We've always been reliant on adaptation; it's nothing new to us. In fact, I think we thrive on fast-paced change. But, for the last eight years or so, we've been constantly beaten over the head with the omnichannel, technology and online sales baton. While important, we've taken our eye off the physical aspect of retail.

Where I think retailers can make the most change now, lies in changing minds, changing perceptions and changing feelings and emotions. These changes most easily take place in an area we have full control over – our own four walls of retail.

The area to focus on is not omnichannel, technology or even digital – it's the physical experiences and interactions that are now a luxury and craved by our increasingly isolated and anxious society. And these experiences can almost be magical. While other retailers are struggling to re-ticket for the next sale that will drop their profit another point, your key to thriving and adapting lies right inside your store every day.

No-one knows your customers like you do. As Emmet from *The Lego® Movie*™ would say, 'You are the special'. In fact, you are the key to unlocking what makes them happy, what challenges them and what keeps them up at night. Either you already know, or you have the power to dig a little deeper.

See, as we'll discuss further in the next chapter, as a retailer it's often counterintuitive to focus on anything that doesn't directly relate to sales. So if, for instance, you sell camping gear, you may be drawn to experiences and events that help you sell more stuff. Instead, however, think of what campers are passionate about. What do they worry about, what do they wonder about and how can you help them curate information and products so that they are drawn to you for advice and expertise? How can you become the go-to place for them on camping? It's a bit of 'roll up your sleeves' work, but the output is worth ten times the input on your part.

THE VALUE OF CUSTOMER ENGAGEMENT

3

By now, you've heard me mention 'customer engagement' several times, and I promise we'll get into exactly what I mean as we work through this book and my Experiment. Engagement itself is a sort of definition, but throughout the book, I'm specifically talking about customer engagement for someone like you – a retailer. So it's retailers' customers we are talking about here.

First, though, you may be wondering, 'What's in it for me?' Sure, in the previous two chapters we've established that customers are changing and that shopping and our in-store environment has changed dramatically due to many factors. *Yup*, you might be thinking, *that all makes sense from what I see in-store. But what can I gain from this?*

A customer who is fully engaged represents an average 23% premium in terms of share of wallet, profitability, revenue, and relationship growth compared with the average customer.

Gallup Customer Engagement Knowledge Center

The folks at Rosetta refer to customer engagement as a personal connection between a consumer and the brand that is strengthened over time, resulting in mutual value. It's an enduring two-way relationship that simultaneously delivers relevant experiences to your customers and greater profitability for your brand.

In a nutshell, customer engagement is about us giving customers what they want, which, in turn, leads to them reciprocating with advocacy, loyalty and, of course, their wallet.

SHOW ME THE MONEY!

As I've already touched on, my Retail Experiment started because I knew something was amiss with my customers, and I knew it wasn't just mine. I'd spoken to other retailers, and they were telling the same story – that, despite more discounting and more money spent on advertising, they were seeing fewer people interested in sales campaigns. In my journey to find answers, the findings from Rosetta's 2014 Customer Engagement Consumer Survey[1] provided some of the first, comprehensive insights, with clear top and bottom line financial benefits.

The report based on this survey pointed directly to customer engagement as helping reduce competitive threat, and create better advocacy, stronger loyalty and increased opportunity for both cross- and upsell. So, naturally, that caught my attention – as I'm sure it would catch yours.

Here are some further details from Rosetta on what customer engagement can mean for your retail business:

- *Stronger loyalty:* Of your highly engaged customers (HECs), 94 per cent describe themselves as loyal, versus 19 per cent of other customers.

- *Reduced competitive threat:* HECs are twice as likely to purchase their preferred brand, even when a competitor has a better deal or lower price.

- *Greater advocacy:* HECs are four times more likely to advocate on behalf of the brand to colleagues and acquaintances.

- *Increased opportunity for upsell and cross-sell:* HECs are six times more likely to say that they would try a new product or service from the brand as soon as it comes out.

As Rosetta sums up,

> As a result, highly engaged customers buy 90% more frequently, spend 60% more per transaction, and have 3x the annual value compared to non-highly engaged customers.

Issues like declining loyalty and increased competitive threat were big issues for my store. While I realise many different types of retailers can relate to these, the home appliance and consumer electronics industry was really in a squeeze. So the kinds of advantages to customer engagement outlined by Rosetta were certainly attractive.

CUSTOMER ENGAGEMENT AND RETAIL

So, now that you understand what's at stake financially, you can better understand what you can gain. It also should be a wake-up call that people want to be engaged – and you stand to lose everything if you choose to ignore them. Your customers crave engagement, and if you are not helping facilitate this engagement, you're likely to lose them to a more sophisticated retailer who can.

Why engagement seems counterintuitive

You're in retail, so you don't need me telling you these are crazy times. One thing that is absolutely predictable, however, is that sales events and 'on sale' messaging is still alive and well. Because, let's face it – retailers exist to sell things, right?

Since the very definition of retail is 'the sale of goods or commodities directly to consumers', I suppose the question I'd like to pose is, how can we challenge the status quo sales strategy? I don't know about you, but I've noticed people just don't like to be sold to anymore. (This connects with the 'new customer', covered in chapter 1.) Except for a few strange people, like myself, most people despise being sold to. We want a story, we want to feel good – we don't want to be *sold* to.

Let's assume you agree with me (throw me a bone here) that people are not as receptive to being sold to as they once were. Why then, as retailers, are we so hell-bent on continuing to run all those screaming commercials – offering interest-free terms with 40 per cent off, this weekend only!!! Why do we focus so heavily on handling customer objections and closing the sale? That sounds like 'sales speak' to me.

What I'm about to share with you in the following parts of this book is a real account of what I did and how I did it – and also the fantastic results it had for my retail business. I know this is the next big evolution of retail and I'm hoping by the end of the book you'll agree it not only works but also is a much more civilised and personally fulfilling way to grow your retail business.

I think it's also important to point out that loads of 'retail consultants' are out there willing to give you their two cents. However, many of these people have never owned a retail store, let alone worked in one. Retail is a tough gig and, while people working outside of our world often think it's all fun and games and loads of money, it's actually a pretty demanding and stressful career.

My advice is to never underestimate your personal knowledge of your customers. Big data has a major role and can give us snapshots of what's working and where we are falling down. Engaging customers in-store, however, gives you live access to real people talking about real problems and solutions. While big data is an awesome side dish, aim to get your main course of input from customers in-store and embrace the little experiments along the way.

MY FIRST 'ENGAGEMENT' EXPERIMENT

I'd like to share with you one of my most positive stories about customer engagement, which happened when I was searching for ways to re-engage with our customer base. I'd been retailing for over nine years at this point, but noticed our marketing ROI shrinking quite considerably. I also noticed our profit was deteriorating and felt a significant change was happening that was inhibiting our messaging. Or perhaps the messaging was now wrong. Either way, I set out to find some answers on why we were spending more than ever on marketing but getting less and less of the 'action' in our call-to-action marketing.

I found that one of the most strained parts of our retail story was plain old disengagement from customers. In other words, we'd send emails out announcing we had a special event on … Yup, crickets. I was in appliance retailing and people just didn't trust us. In fact, I think our trust level was about one step above that of a used car salesman (sorry guys). Customers constantly shopped us for a price and seemed very disengaged once they entered the store. It's disheartening when you have amazing staff and a focus on customer service but are not even given the opportunity to prove yourself.

So I decided to give people a reason to come in and experience the non-self-centred, generous and playful side of retail. We had some fantastic staff and I invited some experts in nutrition and cooking to come in-store to prepare some delicious yet healthy food, and talk about all the benefits that foods high in nutrition have for the body and mind.

I briefed the staff that I would take this night out of their commission structure. This night was not about selling; it was about giving back to the customers. In fact, all of our cashiers had left, and the tills weren't even open (which I found later to be a bit of a mistake). As I delivered this heartfelt speech to my staff, I could feel their eyes rolling into the backs of their heads with disbelief – and I'm sure they thought I'd gone mad.

Despite the pushback and doubt, I persisted. All of my years in sales training, marketing and retail, however, would not prepare me for what happened next. Because we weren't selling things, our customers were in awe of our efforts and genuinely thankful. They lined up after the nutrition and cooking workshop like the receiving line in a scene from *My Big Fat Greek Wedding*, wanting to tell me what a fun and entertaining evening they'd had. Many asked when another workshop would be on and asked if they would be invited. I asked these customers what other kinds of things they were interested in and I got tonnes of feedback. So I asked for their email addresses and started a very plain, non-marketing conversation with them about what was happening in-store and how we'd like to invite them back.

Now the reason I've started this chapter out with my first engagement experiment is because I think it's important to point out that my first test wasn't perfect, but I was trying to do something differently because I felt what we were doing wasn't working.

As we move through the book, you'll no doubt jot down ideas and action points. Just note that they might not always be 100 per cent because we are pioneers in this area. The value of engagement is well documented, and big firms like Deloitte, Rosetta and PWC have metrics for measuring customer engagement. However, the problem is that even these big-time experts don't know how retailers can go about implementing these ideas. But they do know how to measure them.

So here's what we do know: we know that engagement comes from giving with no intention of receiving. I'm sure you've told your kids or other children that when they give something, what they get back isn't important; what is important is the thought behind the gift and the joy that comes from giving to others. And I can hear your inner cynic from here, asking, 'What dream world is she living in? These are tough times that call for tough measures.' I agree with you. I started these experiments at the tail end of the global financial crisis (GFC), so I'm familiar with tough measures. In fact, doing what's right has always taken a lot more guts than going with the flow. But I warn you: a lot of retailers are going with the flow, and if you're not prepared to try something different, you might just find yourself being quickly outpaced and out-manoeuvred.

SO WHAT'S CUSTOMER ENGAGEMENT ALL ABOUT?

Customer engagement is all about creating experiences that encourage your customers to interact with you and then share the experiences that you create for them. The creation of these experiences is not to extract *revenue* but rather to create *value*.

This world is full of people and companies that want to sell us things. To be honest, we don't need any more of these people. What we need are businesses and retailers that we can trust for advice, that we feel comfortable visiting and that overall deserve our dollars. We need more retailers who not only make a decent living but are also decent human beings. If I can be quite matter of fact and to the point: if this doesn't resonate with you on some level, this book really isn't for you.

I owned a large appliance store, and our customers came from all walks of life. They weren't hoity-toity shoppers, but just your average middle-class Australians. As with any marketing, it was vital to deliver relevant information to these customers – even if it was *free*. As you'll see in the following sections, depending on your customers and their needs, these interactions might be free, or they might have a cost associated. Either way, these interactions need to be right for your customers and made specifically for them only.

WHO ARE YOUR IDEAL CUSTOMERS AND WHAT ARE THEIR PROBLEMS?

First off, I want to get you thinking about your customers, and about solving real and meaningful problems for them. Possible solutions might not even have anything to do with your products. This might seem a bit foreign, but just trust the process. What kinds of problems do we as humans have?

Our most basic problems usually revolve around not enough:

- time

- money

- knowledge.

If you can solve one or multiple problems relating to these areas in a meaningful and helpful way, you've probably got something valuable to offer your customers.

 ## TIME OUT: YOUR IDEAL CUSTOMERS AND THEIR PROBLEMS

Grab a piece of paper and brainstorm some ideas right now. Ask yourself these questions:

1   What does my ideal customer look like? (*Hint:* You might have three or more already established personas for your brand. Just pick one at a time, and then repeat this process for each persona.) Give your ideal customer a name (for example, John or Janet).

2   What really frustrates this person? What do they wish they had more or less of? (*Hint:* Frustrations could include not having enough time with family, partner being away, their job, not feeling they are providing for their family, not saving money or being overweight.)

3   What do they fear? (*Hint:* Fears could include losing their job, not being the best parent, poor health, being sick or dying.)

4   What do they wish they could do, but aren't doing now? (*Hint:* Goals could include losing weight, being more organised, getting fit, cooking healthier meals, improving their technology skills, or selecting clothes and a style that suits them and their body type.)

FOCUSING ON VALUE FOR CUSTOMERS

Only once you understand your customers' problems – or at least try to understand them – can you suggest or find valuable solutions for them. Only after you've done some brainstorming on what sorts of problems your customers have, can you understand how you might add some value to their lives by solving some or even just part of their problems.

One way you might gain greater insight into these problems is through customer surveys. However, it should also be noted that just because they've handed over their problems, your value to them is not necessarily implicitly stated. Steve Jobs once said, 'It's really hard to design products by focus groups. A lot of times, people don't know what they want until you show it to them.' (Replacing the word 'products' with 'experiences' would cover our purposes here as well.)

As an example of this, following my first engagement test (outlined earlier in this chapter) several people asked for cooking classes, yet when cooking classes were announced, we had low attendance and interest. However, when we decided to look specifically at certain lifestyles and cooking topics – like Paleo or raw cooking – the interest was at least 70 per cent higher. Mind you, not one person in our first experiment group mentioned they would like a Paleo or raw cooking workshop, but those were the topics that happened to have the most attendance in the early days.

As we progress down this yellow brick road to *value*, we gain further insights from customers and are rewarded with more trust and reciprocity. We're heading in the right direction of engagement, but it doesn't happen overnight.

This is why I say that customer engagement is counterintuitive to retailers. We don't naturally think this way – we are self-centred for the most part. While we love a great in-store sales event, if we slip back to the 'it's all about me' attitude and try to sell while giving value, it's perceived as trickery and it will do more harm than good.

TIME OUT: ADDING VALUE STEP #1

Revisiting your customers' problems again, think a bit further on how you could add value for the problems you've uncovered. Run through the following:

1   Specify each persona using the name you gave them (that is, John or Janet, or whatever name you chose).

2   Thinking about their frustrations, what are some educational, inspirational or memorable experiences that might help them overcome these frustrations? What are some ways to help solve their frustrations? (*Hint:* If they are frustrated about the level of stress in their lives, for example, think about topics that help relieve stress, such as yoga, meditation and exercise.)

3   Thinking about their fears, what are some educational, inspirational or memorable experiences that might put their minds at rest? (*Hint:* If they were fearful of not being a good enough parent, for example, think about topics that might help them, such as nutrition for kids, toddlers and sleep, and dealing with temper tantrums.)

4   Thinking about the items you listed under what they want to do but aren't doing now, what are some strategies for helping them become more motivated to do those activities? (*Hint:* If a goal you identified was to lose weight, think about topics that might help them with this, such as insights into food preparation, nutrition info, getting active and exercising techniques.)

MARKETING MESSAGES, DEPOSITS AND WITHDRAWALS

A classic psychology technique in relationships is the metaphor where each party has a bank account. In this metaphor, the favours and nice things we do for our significant others are attributed as 'deposits' – when we do something lovely, we are making a 'deposit' into their bank account. If we forget a birthday, do something selfish or say something hurtful, we are making a 'withdrawal' from our partner's bank account.

Each one of these deposits and withdrawals is noted by the other partner. We don't keep a personal ledger, of course, but in many ways, we know exactly where we stand – and whether or not we are in the dog house.

You can also think of your relationships with your customers in this fashion. You sending them an email asking them to come in and buy stuff from you is a 'withdrawal'. Don't be fooled into thinking that because you've offered them 30 per cent off, it's some kind of a deposit from you – it's not. If we are actually honest with ourselves and analyse our activities, we find we tend to make lots of withdrawals and very few deposits.

As I covered in chapter 1, our customers' expectations and our goal posts have significantly changed. At the height of the advertising age, we were impressed by smart marketing and flattered by the newfound interest in our wallets, but now we demand more and need more to keep us interested. On some level, we are aware of the deposits and withdrawals and won't be taken advantage of.

Bring this awareness to your business. When you contact customers, remember they are people, and they will reciprocate or purchase either when you've made enough deposits, or when you've completely stripped off all profit, and they know you're offering the best price.

Wouldn't you rather make regular deposits that could genuinely help them in real and meaningful ways, than constan' them with a price that sacrifices your entire profit margin? This realisation is where customer engagement starts.

THE FACEBOOK RABBIT HOLE

Pretend for a moment you're Alice. I'll be the rabbit and encourage you to follow me down a rabbit hole. Imagine being young and at a university campus (oh, this is quite fun!). Now try to imagine for a moment what the initial conversations about Facebook might have been back in 2003 and 2004.

Mark Zuckerberg is sitting down and pitching his idea about people 'connecting' online, and how his platform brings people 'together' with posts about what was happening in their life. At the time, people were probably thinking, *What? That's the stupidest thing I've ever heard. Why wouldn't they just tell their friends or call them?* It's hard to put yourself in that place because Facebook is sooooo huge, but if you've ever had to pitch a new idea or concept, you'll understand where I'm coming from. Sometimes the most counterintuitive ideas are the best.

Customer engagement is very similar in that it too seems to go against a retailer's better instincts. Historically, to be a good retailer you need to be focused on closing the sale, on listing the features and benefits, on building rapport. Overall, you needed to be focused on selling. After all, the whole point of having your business is to sell your products, provide excellent customer service and to outperform the other retailers selling similar things. Right? It's time to switch this old way of thinking, as comfortable as it may seem, and focus more on delivering value rather than extracting revenue from your customers.

It's time to fill up your customers' senses and emotions and engage them. Get them to stand up and take notice of you through amazing experiences and worthwhile content and support. So let's get started!

All life is an experiment. The more experiments you make the better.

Ralph Waldo Emerson

Part II
THE RETAIL EXPERIMENT

This part of the book lays out my situation in the appliance and electronics industry and how my Retail Experiment began. As I outline this case, however, please keep referring back to your own unique retail environment.

The Retail Experiment is not specific to my retail industry, but the facts and historical sharing I offer are necessary to show what I did in my own retail business. Since 'The Experiment', I've seen all kinds of retailers benefit from offering similar in-store experiences and also from experimenting within their own stores.

And don't worry – once I outline my situation and Retail Experiment, parts III to VII take you through doing your own experiment and the strategies you can incorporate in your store to wake up, re-engage and excite your customers.

THE PERFECT
STORM

4

People most often refer to the 'perfect storm' as a rare combination of catastrophic events, but here I refer to it as more of a positive set of circumstances that opened my retailer eyes. The events combining for my perfect storm were the retail environment, trends in centralising and nationalising stores, my newly discovered engagement and events research, as well as my history and skills. These created the perfect combination of both retail discovery and deceit.

In this age of the customer, the only sustainable competitive advantage is knowledge and engagement with customers.

Forrester

REACHING OUR HIGHEST POTENTIAL

I suppose some might call this perfect storm destiny; others may say that 'everything happens for a reason'. I think my personal favourite explanation is from Aristotle, who believed that not only is the universe in a state of motion, but also at the same time a definite constant exists. His constant was called 'entelechy' – which loosely translates to 'your unique-to-you highest potential'. See, Aristotle believed that everyone on the planet possessed within themselves their own ability to reach their highest potential – which is kind of cool, when you think about it. According to Aristotle, inside each of us – if (as he points out) we listen and act – this 'entelechy' drives us to discover and make changes so we can reach our own highest potential.

Don't get me wrong; I don't feel as though I've reached my highest potential yet – not by far. But I do think it was this 'entelechy' (or what could also be called the 'perfect storm') that led me to explore changing customer behaviours. Included in the mix was a dash of my prior experience, stirred with trends in retailing structures and what I saw inside our store. Combined, this drove me to uncover and seek out more answers.

MY RETAIL ENVIRONMENT – THE LOWDOWN

Although solving problems was at the heart of my experiment, you should be familiar with the retail environment leading up to it. It was late 2012 and, although the GFC had officially kicked off in 2008, we were still feeling the aftermath. Our sales were finally recovering, but not nearly as quickly as we had hoped.

Our store was 2500m², so we had plenty of overheads as a JVP (joint venture partner) of The Good Guys, which was then an independent appliance and electrical retailer. Because our organisation didn't have public investors to contend with – and we had a partner who gave us a lot of autonomy – we pretty much ran our store as if it were our own baby (within, of course, the confines of our partnership agreement on marketing and operations). So what follows here is in no way a 'dig' at The Good Guys – in many ways, we were very contemporary compared to our competitors.

These observations, while specific details may vary from retailer to retailer, are stock standard.

To give you an idea of size and performance, The Good Guys chain at the time had around 109 stores, and we typically sat at around twentieth or so for our sales and profitability. While we didn't have the volume or population of some of the larger city stores (that beat us in those figures) or the low marketing costs of the regional stores, we did pretty well for being outside a city, still having to pay the larger metropolitan advertising costs, yet residing in the far suburbs.

With each campaign – whether it was a television or radio campaign, or catalogue letterbox drop – we would see a definite spike in sales and store visitation. Like all retailers, regardless of their product offering, our day-to-day activities all worked around a cyclical and seasonal theme. In summer, we'd offer things appealing to hot days, during winter we'd similarly offer appropriate products, and so on. Our campaigns were all built primarily around price and product offerings and sales. In the next part, we will talk more about why this doesn't serve our customers in the best possible way; however, for now just recognise that all retail inherently follows similar patterns of 'on sale' and 'off sale' periods that revolve around seasonal campaigns.

One day, as I was microwaving my lunch in our break room, our manager Dan was sharing a story with a couple of others about how their customer had just driven 60 kilometres for a $25 price match from a competitor. This story wasn't the first I'd heard, but I felt it was the start of a new era.

Soon, this same type of story would be shared at industry meet-ups and trade days. Staff would gather round and try to one-up each other with stories of customers getting four or five different quotes to end up saving about $20 on a $2000 to $2500 purchase. Time after time, the inevitable moral of the story seemed to be that surely the customer's time was worth more than $20 and driving to five different stores and wasting over three hours of their time.

Later on, of course, our campaigns also included raising our online profile and highlighting our e-commerce offerings. To start with, we'd give customers gift cards or percentage-off incentives for purchasing online from us, funded by our partner and head office. However, after the glamour and excitement played out, we were expected to fund the incentives from our individual P/Ls, and many of the offers were below cost.

While e-tailing was necessary to reduce future competitive threats and indicated to our customers our helpful and adaptive nature, many of our competitors resisted getting involved and were late to the party. However, while we were ahead of our rival national competitors in comparison, carts and technology, globally, we were all behind the eight ball.

As self-fulfilling prophecies go, our incentives and discounts worked. Our e-commerce was going off – finally, the Australian consumer had embraced buying appliances and electronics online, and our competitors were forced to follow suit. I suppose a celebration was in order, right?

TRENDS IN CENTRALISING AND THE NATIONALISING OF MARKETING

When I first started off in marketing for The Good Guys in 2003, we had about 40 people in the head office; however, during the 'Experiment' years, head office had swelled to over 420 people. As you can imagine, with a 'support centre' of this size, our fees had increased as well.

In the years before this, most stores would have had a local area marketing person who would liaise directly with the head office marketing team and also spearhead local initiatives with other businesses and local promotional campaigns. However, those days were long gone. The upstairs offices at my store – which used to house marketing, merchandisers, buyers and back-office administration – were now empty, ghost-like cubicles. As the days passed, we seemed to become less and less responsible for our success and more in the hands of our head office. Our staff now consisted of cashiers, warehouse and sales staff, and a couple of managers across the teams.

At the same time, we were forming a national partnership with Jamie Oliver and sinking heaps of money into his 'Ministry of Food Australia' presence. I loved Jamie. (I mean, who doesn't really? He's such a lovable guy with a fantastic message.) And we were in the midst of launching giant semitrailer trucks across Australia so Jamie could get his message out to those areas that were disadvantaged, starting with the most overweight areas in Australia – with our area second on the list. (More on how this partnership with Jamie played out, and its influence on my Retail Experiment, in chapter 11.)

In addition to all the cause-related marketing now engulfing our marketing budgets, we were also putting bucketloads of money into our advertising campaigns. It was as if the whole of our industry was in a major competition for who could waste the most advertising dollars.

In the past, we had prided ourselves on our lean advertising budgets – at one time, I recall seeing a statistic that indicated we spent six times less in advertising than our closest competitor. We were proud of the fact that we didn't have to advertise as much and sort of looked down our noses at those retailers forced to advertise just to get the people through the door.

Now, however, our fully centralised marketing team argued we had to spend more money to grow market share. So, as the story goes, we forged ahead, making no note whatsoever of our failing campaigns or decreasing visitation rates. It seemed the only thing left to do was spend more on the very thing that was no longer working.

It was during this very frustrating time that I became extremely curious about what was going on with our customers. Why were they becoming so fickle and so disengaged? We weren't doing anything that differently, yet our customers were definitely cooling off and becoming more and more distant.

So being the owner, inquisitive marketer and science nerd that I am, I asked around among my colleagues. They too confirmed something strange was afoot. Customers were becoming very price-conscience, and I soon realised this wasn't unique to our store. One thing I could identify as having changed significantly was that we were engaging in more and more push marketing, and we were focusing less on being the local hero. See, while The Good Guys was a national brand, our names were on the front of each store in bright lights. Everything we did was under our name, but our local area market (LAM) budgets were reduced and our national marketing budgets were growing and growing.

As well as a marketer and science nerd, I was also a lover of psychology and retail, and I decided something was lacking. What did the Apple store have, and what did stores like Williams-Sonoma have? These guys were all offering an amazing in-store experience, and I also had an interest in this area and events. When marketing was centralised into The Good Guys head office, we still had several statewide events and partnerships that needed managing. I put my hand up in those very early days to organise and manage some large awards nights and industry events we were part of. While events were not something I knew a lot about at the time, I enjoyed the large budgets, marketing and the fun and creative side. Through managing and hosting these events, I also saw how, in just a few short years, we got some serious respect and admiration from our suppliers.

I started to suspect that we were definitely lacking in our events and in-store experience, so I set off to research and find what was happening in Australia and around the world. What were the world-class retailers doing? How could I start leveraging some of the strategies they used in my store?

ENGAGEMENT AND ITS VALUE ...

I run through my research into the value of customer engagement in chapter 3, so my focus here is how my findings related to my store. It quickly became apparent to me that we had little if any metrics on our in-store engagement. I also recognised my customers as I researched the attributes of a disengaged customer. Now armed with how valuable engaged customers were, I set out on a mission to find out how to re-engage them.

Interestingly enough, if you Googled 'customer experience' back in 2013 and 2014, about 98 per cent of the results would have been on the digital customer experience. Almost no data was available on the world wide web on the in-store customer experience.

Of course, digital was big guns then – they were having significant, double-digit growths year on year and our organisation was embracing the market early and often. Every campaign had a digital component and, while I could see it was a learning curve and sales were continually on the rise, I felt we were 'baiting' customers with online offers for no real gain other than to show them how easy it was. Most of the offers made were just to get customers to consider buying online from us, and involved very skinny or zero profit.

My next research interest – covered in length in part IV on humanics – was the impacts of digital versus human interaction. To have researched this at all just seems silly now, but given no information was available on the web about the in-store experience, I thought perhaps my 'gut feeling' of human interactions being stronger than online was wrong. Surely, some retail experts would have posted information about strategies and tactics to engage and interact with people inside the store as being at least as important as interacting digitally? At the time, I couldn't find anything.

The full findings of my research are found in part IV, but the main point to mention here is the psychological data and results I found, later on, supported the idea that human or personal interaction trumps anything that digital can cook up – yes, even virtual reality. And the most powerful interaction could come through events.

EVENTS WERE MAGICAL LITTLE BITS OF EMOTIONAL ENGAGEMENT

While I was researching customer engagement and the in-store experience, I also thought back to the events I had organised earlier. And I realised the awards and the supplier–industry events were magical little bits of emotional and everlasting memories. Sure, other similar events were held in our industry, but none really put the people calling on us 'on show' so to speak and rewarded them for their partnership and dedication to growing our business. Many years later, people would still approach me to talk about the amazing experience they had at the event, and how grateful they were but also that they were invited to attend.

This realisation really got me thinking about how influential and special events and experiences are to people. I wondered what was happening in those particular events that transformed individuals and ideas. What were the strategies or important 'bits' that really converted a typical event into a major influencer of an industry? More importantly, how could we utilise this emotional engagement machine for our retail customers?

So my first step in the Retail Experiment journey was to capture the magic behind these events. I sat down over a Sunday and mapped out all the moving parts of our successful awards and industry events, specifically noting down the emotional, memorable and influential things that affected our guests the most. The following sections outline what I noted as the most influential.

Human-to-human experiences

First off, events by their very nature are human-to-human experiences. While you can have tech to help get ideas and concepts across to people and, I suppose, 'wow' your attendees, overall the event is all about people coming together to celebrate, learn, inspire or acknowledge other people. In other words, an awards webinar wouldn't have the same impact as an event that brought people together for a common cause.

Easy to communicate and share socially

Secondly, the event theme or what it was about means there's always heaps of pictures and opportunities for social sharing. After all, people have gotten onto planes, and into cars and Ubers to come and spend time at the event. They are dressed and primed and ready to let their friends, colleagues and families know they're there and they like it. Okay, good, that's also helpful to retail. To increase our impact, we need to be mindful about the narrative, and about the picture or experience that can be shared out to a broader network – reaching more than just the people at the event.

All about the attendees

Another observation I jotted down was that the events we put together were all about the attendees. Our awards night had a short speech from the state chairmen, but even that was simply to thank and acknowledge the amazing suppliers in the room who helped us become so successful. Everything else – and I mean everything – was for the benefit of our suppliers.

Our credo for all decisions involving this event was, 'How does that benefit the supplier?' In short, if it didn't directly benefit the supplier or their partner (guest), it didn't happen.

As the influence of these events grew, I shared the historical importance (and great results) of focusing on our attendees. From then on, we were absolutely focused on the *beneficiary* of these events – the attendees. Often, other owners would have some input for future awards or events. Our standard question when assessing these suggestions was always how does that additional expense benefit the supplier or their partner? If there was not a direct and positive impact or benefit, it simply didn't happen.

In social psychology, reciprocity is a rule that says people should repay, in kind, what another person (or, in our example, organisation) has provided for them – that is, people give back (reciprocate) the kind of treatment they have received from another.

This is exactly what happened in our case. We didn't set out to get anything back in return, it just happened.

Advocacy

Advocacy was another thing all of our events had in common. After a representative was short-listed to attend, which was based on performance and voted on by all the store owners, they were very excited. Both before and after the event, it was an assumed bragging right with your colleagues. Also, if you happened to make the podium for an award on the night, you were really well respected within our industry.

Nick, a well-known rep in our industry, provides an example of the respect that came from gaining one of our awards. He was amazing at his role and, therefore, won the Most Valuable Representative of the Year Award three times in a row. He said he was given a raise each year after winning the award and was finally headhunted by a rival brand to take on a national sales role. So the benefits for attendees and award-winners were not only social (within their organisations) but also financial.

Community and cause

I also noted that broad events never had the same vibe as niched ones. Having a group of like-minded individuals together in itself was magical. When the event was smaller and more niched, attendees had even more in common – and these were the events that provided the most magic.

Returns and benefits

As mentioned, we gave out trophies, accolades and awards, invited spouses and partners, and even had professional photographers there to take photos of attendees and their partners so they could remember the night for years to come.

All in all, these were fairly expensive endeavours; however, the returns were huge. We reinforced an amazing connection with the very people supplying our products – and, therefore, the pricing of products in-store. In the first few years of holding the events, we noticed a big change in cooperation – it was as if we were now finally partners working together for a common goal.

When we planned new campaigns, stock was low or product training was needed, our state and organisation was always looked after first in our industry. In fact, even other states within our organisation didn't get the amazing benefits that we did because of these unique events.

Onwards and upwards ...

After reflecting on the power of the past events I had been involved with, and armed with the research on engagement I shared in the previous chapter, I became almost obsessed with customer engagement, experience and our customer's journey. It was now time to hypothesise, test, hypothesise again and move forward with what I knew was a new retail frontier.

So despite having no real evidence-based information pertaining to retail engagement, I was off – to test and to find a way to re-engage our customers through the in-store customer experience. I had no intention then to write a book or to share my information with others. I was simply looking for answers to my very own real problems.

HYPOTHESIS, OBSERVATIONS AND EPIC FAILS

5

You know how you can really get into something new, like a diet – say, no sugar or low-carbs – and then, before you have even succeeded yourself, you start telling all your colleagues and friends they should do it too? Yeah, that was totally me. It was as if Christmas had come early and I was trying to save my colleagues and retail friends. I'm fairly sure in the early days they thought I was crazy (and I probably was for sharing waaaaay too early) but my heart was in the right place. We had a great group of retailers who were passionate and clever, and yet were somehow struggling to connect to their customers. We had to do something.

Within months, I had stacks of statistics, research and our own customer survey data. I felt ready to step out and officially test my

> When something is important enough, you do it even if the odds are not in your favour.
>
> *Elon Musk*

hypothesis on improving engagement through great in-store customer experiences.

Initially I was most excited about the possible physical and sensory experiences. I contacted several of our proactive suppliers with interesting products and asked if they would take part in a special one-off event in our store to really put the products 'on show' for two special hours. The idea was to have little 'mini-shows' for each product, only lasting a few minutes each to help give customers bite-sized information.

Back then, my ideas were really about giving little bits of value in a convenient way, with the idea that people could stop in to the store whenever it was convenient for them to learn and experience different products. The following figure shows the 'handmade' in-store flyer passed out on the night (Unfortunately, I don't have the actual advert I used in the local press.) You can get an idea of some of the 'experiences' available on the night from the flyer.

FAILURE BEFORE SUCCESS

Unfortunately, this event was *not* a runaway success. First of all, the offer to the customers was not strong enough and was way too generic. The advert revolved around the whole idea of experiencing the products, and included models/products and pricing information – with few call outs of the 'experience' offered. A quick look at my notes for what made events magical little bits of emotional engagement would have shown me I was missing two essential parts – the event was not all about the attendee and I wasn't talking to a specific community within our store, but the whole database. However, that's how we learn from our mistakes. I remembered that list I had drawn out several months earlier, looked it over and went back to the drawing board.

Not long after this 'Experience Night', we had a special announcement of a new kitchen offering. We were the first pilot store to partner with kitchen cabinet makers to build or renovate an entire kitchen. This was a new service that provided a one-stop-shop to our customers.

Because we were the first store, no nationalised branding or rollout was yet available. So, with this new, uncharted launch event on the horizon, I went into full experience, event and marketing mode. Before Dropbox or any other file-sharing apps were mainstream, I produced a full video as the invite – and hand-mailed postcards with a USB containing the video attached. This invitation was sent off to the mayor, local councillors, journalists, fellow business owners and influencers in our local area. (The image on the following page shows the postcard, with attached USB, and its envelope.)

The invitation was a funny throw back to a Bob Dylan video with flash cards – promising a sneak peak of the very first Good Guys kitchen launch in Australia, complete with chefs, champagne, canapés and a bit of education for all those who attended. I purposely briefed the chef and asked him to divulge two or three secret chef tips for making canapés for guests in your home.

We had a fantastic turnout for this, but what was even more significant to the overall Experiment was how influential the invitees were in promoting and advocating locally for this event. We were covered in every newspaper, and on the websites for the local council and local radio stations. Other businesses contacted us to find out if they could bring managers. The day before the event, our local radio station wanted to come shoot video for their website. And one of our guests even wrote about her experience at the event in her blog, which was followed by many of the locals in the community. The majority of people were really surprised by the gracious tips our chef divulged and how fun it was – for example, Mark, a local businessman, said, 'Honestly, I came for some bubbly and to support you guys but I was blown away with how personal it was and how much I learned while I was here tonight. It was really a great evening.'

While you probably have your own strengths, mine was marketing. Having had experience as a national and global marketer, I had a deep appreciation for style guides and standardising branding. I was not a big fan of rogue marketers producing their own dodgy things – it needed to be perfect after all!

But the beauty and success of this event made it evident to me that on that one night, *we* – our one-store business – we were the super-stars. The people stood up and took notice of what we had to say for once. People were actually talking in town about how great the event was, and how funny my husband was – and they shared it all far and wide on social media. I think it was meaningful to those attendees that they got to know us – some even happened to like us. It was the first time I realised how much more powerful 'going rogue' could be.

THE EXPERIMENT BEGINS ...

Historically in our industry, we had relied on our suppliers to supply demonstrators and reps to help out with sales events. After the kitchen's launch, I started fishing around with interested suppliers, asking for their help with our first in-store events. I'd brief them heavily on a particular product – like, for instance, blenders – and ask them to provide more tips and tricks than just talking about 'features and benefits' of the blender itself. For example, I'd ask for them to provide tips on making green smoothies or nut butters.

Soon, however, I realised asking them to do this was not only unfair but also just not in their DNA. These people were hired for the sole purpose of selling and their very demeanour was exactly the opposite of what I was after – a non-selling, value-adding expert.

First breakthrough

My first real breakthrough came when I met a raw foods chef who ran her own cafe in our local area. When I asked if she was interested in presenting her skills in my shop, she said she was thrilled to have the opportunity to share her vast knowledge with our customers. And she was very well received – so much so we had her come back on five different occasions as the seasons changed and she had new recipes and techniques to share.

Our health-conscious customers were over the moon – they sent emails, posted on social media and talked to me and our staff at length after the presentations. They were excited with how generous the chef was with her training and tips. Later on, I'd see them still lingering in the store looking at products and buying items that the chef was using, like food processors, blenders, dehydrators and other kitchen tools. I could tell I was onto something, but with limited space and limited people interested in raw food, I wasn't sure if it was worth all the trouble of setting her up in store, creating email campaigns and buying her ingredients.

Our success at in-store events builds

Still, I soldiered on, next meeting Leah – the Paleo expert I first mention in chapter 2 – in an entrepreneurial group I was part of. This expert had just started her journey and was looking for ways to increase her reach, and grow her blog and social media following. For mutual benefit, we decided to work together and, soon after her first presentation, I realised what a great decision that was. I realised what she had presented – and how she had presented it – was pretty close to the same 'magic' of our events with suppliers (covered in the previous chapter).

So, in true geek-out, science-nerd fashion, I went back to the list I had created of the most influential factors in creating 'magic moments' at events, comparing the two (very different in style) events, point for point:

- *Human-to-human experiences:* Yes, tick!

- *Easy to communicate and share socially:* Yes, we even had our own hashtags and encouraged checking in and sharing.

- *All about the attendees:* Yes, these were shows that educated and gave people insight into how to start a new Paleo journey. I briefed my expert that while she was to *use* our products, she was only to talk about them if a person asked any questions.

- *Advocacy:* Yes, I immediately saw heaps of sharing and interaction on social media, and inviting of friends and family members to the next presentation.

- *Community and cause:* Yes, tick! The people who attended were all very similar – they had either dabbled in Paleo or wanted to get more info to get started. In fact, I'd learned that many had an autoimmune disease, which was what had interested them in Paleo in the first place.

First engagement and sales wins

Our next step was tracking the sales, engagement and advocacy that we created. Because it was my store, this was a little easier, and I was able to cross-reference attendees with my customer database.

Here's some of the metrics we saw in the first quarter:

- Products selected by attendees were around 6 per cent higher gross profit than our other average sales in that category. Attendees were selecting the better, higher quality products, which had bigger ticket values and better profit because Leah was using them.

- Our visitation rates increased on our event days to around 11 per cent.

- Around 24 per cent of all attendees purchased something in the next five days after an event.

- Sales increases of 5 to 8 per cent on the event day.

- Open rates of emails after a attending an event were sitting at around 75 per cent – pretty much unheard of in the electronic direct mail (EDM) world and a strong indicator of engagement.

Of course, as a franchisee or a corporate store, you might not have access to the same level of information that your head office does. While this was a disadvantage for us as well, we decided to work around it. For each of the experts we used at our events, I started using their social media and tags – and they were more than happy to share the results with me.

Because each retailer has a different POS system, sales reports, and social and visitation reports, it's probably irrelevant to go into how we tracked our success internally. The main point is that we recorded our figures where we could and attributed them to increased visitation, sales, profit and overall advocacy.

In the early days it felt a bit like *Planes, Trains and Automobiles* to get the info (in that we chopped and changed and grabbed whatever info we could), but I knew there was some magic there. We could tell by the looks on people's faces after events that they were happy, totally engaged and extremely appreciative for the lovely experiences we were putting on for them. And, ya know what? It made me feel great, too – like for the first time in quite a while we were responsible for our own success, like we were helping our customers and they actually appreciated it. Who knew?

IT'S ALIVE! *ALIVE!*

6

As I tested and then created my little 'experience monster' it truly did come to life. Not in a scary way, but it just took on a life of its own. Just like you probably would, the retailer in me panicked slightly as this happened, wanting to have complete control. But the marketer in me knew that while I wanted to curate the experiences from start to finish, it was pretty cool that people were getting involved with this workshop long after they left my store. So, I'd sit back and keep an eye on the social comments and let it run for a while to see where it would go.

Because I was interested in Paleo personally, I kept up with what Leah – the Paleo expert who ran the event I talk about in the previous chapter – was doing. I even attended

When everything seems to be going against you, remember that the airplane takes off against the wind, not with it.

Henry Ford

a few of the events she did outside of our store. After all, she had a business before she met me and quite often she organised social or paid events. One of these events was a high tea at Pete Evans's restaurant. (Pete Evans is a well-known Paleo celebrity who you likely know as co-host of *My Kitchen Rules*.) It was during one of these events, where I was just another guest, that I finally realised, as a retailer, I had to just let go of the 'experience monster' I created.

These people were continuing the journey that started off at my store. They were happy and had positive memories of our store for introducing them to Paleo. Most of them had already purchased a slew of appliances from us. It was obvious – to me anyway – that if and when they needed anything else we would definitely be their first choice for purchasing it, and that was just going to have to be good enough ... let it go.

Something that started off at our store in the suburbs of Brisbane was turning into a mini localised movement, where real-life people were eating better, preparing their own food and starting to love life again. I remember early on feeling really good that I helped them do that. I also knew that I wanted to keep trying new things to help people – different people – even more. I started to feel pretty good about what was happening. It was the first time I remember feeling that the experiences I was helping to create were a hell of a lot more exciting than just running our retailing business. I guarantee that if you start having your own unique experiences in-store, you'll feel the same way.

LETTING GO

Have you noticed a lot more entrepreneurs lately? Well, maybe it's just me, but I certainly started noticing a lot more – especially after I enrolled in the Key Person of Influence (KPI) business accelerator program. After my first successes with offering experiences in-store, I wanted to take my ideas further in a business sense. I could tell this was something special that could help retailers and also rebuild that valued trust with their customers that had been lost along the way. And the support and knowledge I gained from other entrepreneurs within KPI soon proved I was right.

As I began meeting more entrepreneurs from this new entrepreneurial group I belonged to I could see immediate fits with particular types of retailers. Food and nutrition experts could help retailers with cooking accessories, sport and home appliance stores for instance. Blokey experts in home automation, cars and DIY could be paired up with hardware and auto retailers.

In the early days, this was a sort of interview, followed up with a talk and look at their products and what they could offer my retailers. Early on, I did a lot of work finding the most unusual ideas, methodologies and presenters.

For me, a real breakthrough was the realisation that these entrepreneurs' concepts and ideas were bigger than my store and me. Some of these people were trying to revolutionise healthcare, others were getting to the root cause of psychological triggers for being overweight, and others were trying to save children's lives.

So it was only natural that the impact of the events I helped these entrepreneurs host in my store rippled out, way beyond the confines of my store and my control. I found myself tagged in conversations on social media, brought in for advice as part of a naturally evolving discussion with other experts.

As I've mentioned, when posts like this first started appearing, I was a little paranoid that this was happening outside of our store, and that our social team didn't instigate or track them. But I soon realised that our one store couldn't put a lid on this type of interaction. Consumers today don't want canned responses; they want to know real information from real people who are using the products. We were legitimately offering insightful and life-changing workshops and experiences – for *free*. It was then I realised I finally had to let it go.

THE CALL TO ADVENTURE

Like you, I love retailing. But after eleven years I was getting restless. I felt like what I was doing with the experts was helping not only others but also my bottom line, my stock turns, my visitation and overall interest in our store. And then, among all this positivity, came another sign I was ready for more.

I'd just received a new national campaign rollout that was boring and common. It was what we referred to in our organisation as 'gift with purchase' – buy a product and get a free cookbook. Suddenly I had this sickening feeling in the pit of my stomach. *Really? I* thought. *Is that the best we can do?* While I loved our store, our brand and my colleagues, we – retailers – were going about this all wrong.

I suddenly had this deep desire to start helping my fellow colleagues, so I reached out to other store owners and started asking if they'd be interested in testing out these same shows and in-store events in their stores. And guess what? They were.

Tide was turning

In the past, I'd worked for a big corporate – Maytag – and already went through two mergers with PWC. So, at the same time as the momentum was building behind our in-store events, I was picking up other signs as well. I was pretty confident that all of our stores were being 'prepped' for sale.

I had also just shared my crazy 'in-store events with entrepreneurs' idea with Glen Carlson, one of the KPI founders – that is, my idea of turning this 'experience monster' into an actual business. After hearing my pitch, Glen said to me, 'Amy, it's inspiring, but you'll never know if this idea has legs until you get people in the market – other retailers – to pay for the service.'

So, with change looming in the air, off I went to start up my little experience baby called Retail Rockstars. I left the store in my husband's hands and began my next retail adventure – developing, marketing and sourcing specialised experts for other retailers and then managing the whole retail event for them.

Of course, by this time, our store was doing very well, and many thought I was crazy … again. Seems to be a theme, doesn't it? Why would I want to leave a $28 million retail business to start organising events for retailers? But I was so passionate about changing this relationship between retailers and customers. I could see that, when customers were engaged, they loved retailers. I wanted other retailers to realise not only how good it feels to help people but also the economic benefits of doing so. But I still had a long way to go.

STARTING MY JOURNEY (AND NOT LOOKING BACK)

After officially leaving The Good Guys, I didn't have to worry as much about having a conflict of interest. So, I started right away on building a social, email and customer relationship platform for my new business.

The first official show outside of my store was with a true retailing pioneer, James Brockhurst. He was innovative in every sense and also keen to see how he could start engaging and exciting his customers in-store.

First, we sat down to discuss his personal insights, store metrics and goals. James was kind of health-conscious himself, and we decided that the topics of Paleo and healthy cooking would be a great place to start with his store too.

Just think about how nervous you'd feel about doing something like this with your customers. Well, that's where James was. He shared that he already had a full roster of product demonstrators scheduled each week. Typically, however, only about three to four customers might show up to these events – sometimes none. I think in his own way he was giving me a warning that this might not work – as he looked into my hopeful and ever-excited eyes. This was his way of offering a way out or a reason not to feel gutted if no-one turned up to this first event. I appreciated it and acknowledged his concern, and then told him that if only three people showed up, I'd do all the marketing and advertising – even pay for the food and the expert and the planning for the entire show – for *free*.

There was no turning back now!

Winning combination

Knowing the Paleo shows were a big hit in my store, our first event was locked in. Utilising my own social media along with that of my Paleo experts, we had RSVPs within hours of releasing the event details.

On the same day, I sent off a media release to the local paper in James's area – but by the time they phoned the next day for more details I had to let them know the free workshop was already fully booked and so it was probably unnecessary to run the story. Interested, they wanted to know more about the free Paleo information that Leah was presenting. Soon, she found herself smack dab in a photo shoot – which was perfect exposure for her, and helped to highlight her expertise, credibility and, above all, the next workshop we were already working on.

This was another example of knowledge from previous testing (and failures) coming together. Previously I had tested which types of stories, advertising copy and emails worked best. As a retailer, what do you think would have the most interest for your customers? Is it an event that:

1 features detailed information on both the expert and the retailer

2 mainly features the retailer but announces the purpose of the event and gives a short bio on the expert

3 solely focuses on the expert?

Well, what do you think?

If you guessed number three, you are correct. After testing hundreds of campaigns with email, social media and editorials, I found that by not mentioning the retailer at all, attendance was around 50 to 63 per cent higher. So, even though your first intuition as a retailer is to plaster your name all over the place, this type of exposure in the press for the expert (and the expert alone) was right up our alley.

And because the next event was showcased in the paper, it was fully booked before we had even announced it to James's customers, or advertised it ourselves.

Just like the events in my own store (where I'd always introduced the expert), I now asked James to introduce our Paleo expert. I knew that by introducing the expert or speaker, the owner shows their care and interest in the people who attend that day. In a more general sense, however, this also associates the retailer's brand with the expert. When customers first walked in the doors, the retailer was just a venue; however, when they leave the store at the end, excited about what they've just learned, that psychological association is now transferred to not just the expert but also the retail store owner.

Now that I had 'a paying client', I also developed my first attendee survey. Among several other questions, the survey queried where attendees had heard about the event. Tracked digitally through links and affiliates, we could see where the attendees were coming from.

The figure on the following page shows a graph from my very first report to James. As you can see:

- 31 per cent of attendees found the event through the Facebook advertising I had done

- 21 per cent found the event on Eventbrite

- 17 per cent found the event through the newspaper, with the same percentage hearing about it through the expert's channels (the 'Other' category in the graph shown represented the expert's social media, website or Meetup group)

- 14 per cent said they heard about it in-store via The Good Guys (in-store posters and flyers – no digital).

How did you hear about the show?

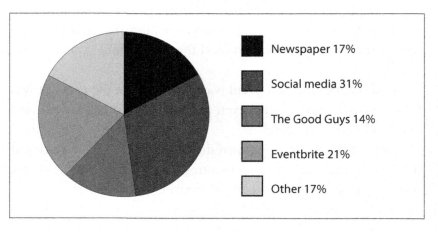

As time rolled on, we strengthened the advertising and the presentations and started working with more and more retailers. The following figures show just a few of the first images we created for the online promotion of shows.

After getting some great numbers on the board for events at other retailers, I started refining the messaging, and started giving back even more to the attendees with follow-up offers and e-books from the 'Rockstars' (the experts). I even added a schmick report to all of our clients that delivered RSVP metrics, attendance figures, marketing mix, feedback on the Rockstar's performance and how likely after seeing this show they'd shop again with this retailer. The following graph lists the responses to this question after an event at Carseldine, for instance.

How likely are you to shop again with this retailer?

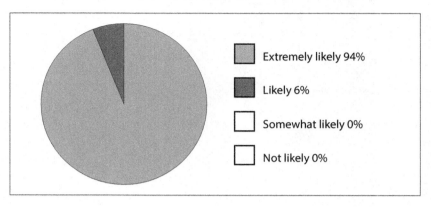

- Extremely likely 94%
- Likely 6%
- Somewhat likely 0%
- Not likely 0%

I also supplied figures to the client on whether attendees had previously purchased at the store (results for the same Carseldine client shown in the following graph). As you can see from the chart, 31 per cent of these attendees had never purchased anything at this store in the past. This rate is quite high for an early show. Previous purchasers as attendees would range anywhere from 12 per cent to this higher rate of 31 per cent. Typically, we'd see a much higher percentage of *new* customers in the first few shows (those who had never purchased at the store). After that, of course, the figures for later shows would settle to around the 15 per cent mark for people who had not purchased in-store before.

Have you purchased here before?

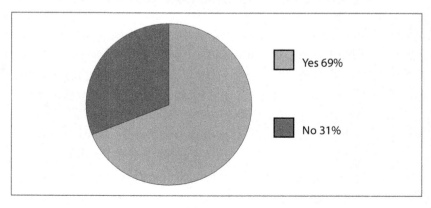

- Yes 69%
- No 31%

A few snags ...

As with any new ideas, we faced a few hiccups along the way. My idea initially, because I was so busy, was to create a service that did not need the owner, franchisee or manager at all. I knew just how busy and full-on running a retail store was and thought, *How great would it be to plan and do all of this without having to 'bother' the 'me' equivalent at all.* I guess, like many, I was creating a service for myself ... I just wanted the job done!

Early on, however, I realised one of the biggest determiners of success with other retailers was how involved the owner was. Store owners who were interested, present and wanting to introduce the experts saw a much better sales ratio, advocacy and overall success.

A couple of different reasons exist for this. First off, those directly involved were much more effective at communicating the vision of in-store events with their staff and suppliers, and that had a direct flow-on effect of letting customers know and pushing the word out even further.

Secondly, those introducing the experts had a unique opportunity to pitch a personalised message to their customers. Simply by introducing the expert or popping their head in for their own in-store event was just like saying to customers, 'Hey, I think you're important, and I like helping you with things you're interested in.'

So, like most things in business, there might be short cuts, but there are no magic pills. While you can leverage your time and money in different ways by always utilising national campaigns, when you decide to step out and do something local, make sure it's personal, and make sure your customers know you're interested in them.

Personally, I didn't think the owner would be so influential on the whole process but, as different owners, franchisees and managers came on, I started seeing a direct correlation with those who were involved and those who weren't.

FINDING YOUR OWN MAGIC

While the experiments in my store and those with my expert Rock-stars might be vastly different to what your customers yearn for, there will be 'something' that resonates deeply with them. And this 'something' is what wakes them up, excites them, motivates them to listen and ultimately draws them into your store.

Experiments are happening all around us every day. Whether they are planned or accidental, our retail environment is telling us something – and what started out as whispers in the late 1990s is now outright screaming.

No-one knows your customers like you. By tapping into your customer insights and research, you too can build your very own experiences.

I'm not sharing my experiment to say I have all the answers, but rather to show you that *you* have all the answers. All I've done is laid out the framework in which I made my discoveries, shown you how I've tested them in other retail environments and walked you through how you too can wake up, engage and excite your disengaged customers.

Now that you have more of an idea on the current statistics, mindset and thought leadership in retail, and how and what I found in my Experiment, the following parts of the book concentrate more on the 'what' and the 'how to'.

Each chapter from here will have some 'Time out' exercises. As you complete each of these chapters, you'll then be able to plug a lot of that work and the findings into the chapters in the final part, which brings all the ideas from the book together and helps you start your unique events and experiences in-store for your own customers. This will form the basis of your very own Experiment and action plan for re-engaging your customers.

By far the most challenging part of experimenting and getting started is finding your unique ideas that will resonate with customers, and then humanising them, telling them and, of course, putting them all together. By completing each part and getting clear about your uniqueness and personalities, what you come up with won't just be 'hypotheses' – they will be a serious short cut to drawing customers to you like magnets and leap-frogging your competition entirely.

Judge a man by his questions rather than his answers.

Voltaire

Part III
BECOMING MORE THAN A SALES MACHINE

STRATEGY ONE: MINDSET

Sometimes it's nice to sit back as if you are a total stranger to your business and observe things for what they are – identifying those historical processes that just keep occurring because that's how they've always been done. As I dug deeper into the heart of customer engagement and experience, I realised our focus was all wrong. If giving back value and empathy were the foundations of customer engagement, I felt we were way off the mark with our constant focus on sales and price messaging. Sure, we had a talented local team who genuinely loved our customers, but more and more I felt as though our national messaging wasn't in line with what this *new* customer really needed.

As I began to dissect our marketing, I identified some rather obvious internal cycles and processes. Initially, I started identifying these processes within my own store and then started comparing them against other similar stores in our state. As similarities grew, I checked them against other states. Finally, I cross-referenced within our industry by checking in with fellow competitors and friends to see if they had similar marketing and sales processes. I wish I could say I stopped there, but it seemed whether I was talking to colleagues who were retailing appliances or friends retailing sunglasses, my discussions and findings all appeared to follow a fairly predictable pattern.

This part is all about helping you as a retailer regain some control through knowledge and awareness. I want to put store owners, franchisees and managers back in the driving seat so they can focus on the customer – which is the ultimate goal we are working towards.

The process here is about moving away from the older 'legacy' mindset, which often obsesses on historical sales events, competitors and suppliers. As we all manoeuvre in an attempt to differentiate ourselves, retailers must realise it's the customers attracted to that difference who will decide our fate.

A little warning: you won't find all your stores' answers in this part. This is just a quick glimpse into the systemic issues facing retailers today. While our problems are real and widespread, some of these decisions might be out of your control and lie in the laps of a head office. Whatever your situation – whether you're a store manager or the owner of an independent store – know that you still have a vital part to play in turning the store around.

INTRODUCING THE SALES MACHINE

7

As I touch on in the introduction to this part, while still at The Good Guys I took a step back to look at the big picture of the appliance and electronic retail marketing. By doing this and talking to other marketers in other retail chains and organisations, I discovered the problems (and possible solutions) were not specific to the appliances and electronics industry – they were widespread across retailing.

After years of deteriorating profit and shrinking return on investment in marketing, I was searching for the missing link. One thing was certain: throwing more money at marketing that wasn't servicing our business or our customers needed to stop. But I just wasn't sure what wasn't working.

> The reason it seems that price is all your customers care about is that you haven't given them anything else to care about.
>
> *Seth Godin*

I did know it was much more of a systemic issue with retail marketing in general – the problems went straight to the core. While messaging had something to do with it, I had this gut-wrenching feeling the problem was bigger than I cared to admit. I was starting to realise everything we focused on and were known for – our whole sales machine – was wrong.

PICTURING THE SALES MACHINE

Let me explain how I uncovered the sales machine, and the problems with it, for our business. Being a very visual person, I envisioned a sprocket-like wheel with cogs while examining this big picture of retail marketing. I pictured it to be cyclical in nature, constantly being driven by products and prices and range. It was updated often based on the latest trends for customers, but also heavily influenced by the marketing from our suppliers. What really stood out the most for me was the constant influence of pricing, products and sale events. I came to see this sprocket-like wheel as the 'sales machine' (see page 111).

Most of our wheel was contributing in some way to driving sales, and scheduling sales events or marketing campaigns – which was ultimately reaching our customer at the end. Procurement lived at the top of the wheel where the beginning of the cycle began. This is where our purchasing teams considered things like trends and replenishment. Pricing was strongly influenced by both the demand of the market and our suppliers.

Next in the cycle was the negotiation of the deals – what was special or noteworthy in the way of price, a gift with purchase or a cash-back deal. As you follow the wheel around, the cycle gets more specific, with detail around specific products, prices and promotions, and where and how they will be communicated with internal staff and potential external customers.

Finally, the last clicks of the wheel are more about the 'how to'. Scheduling and messaging are the main focuses here, including what deals were pre-negotiated and then placed on TV adverts, catalogues, social media campaigns, text messages or staff incentives. This was followed by the final communication of it all with employees.

All of this happens in a very routine fashion. As each campaign concludes, the whole thing starts all over again at the very top.

As a retailer, you might be wondering why I'm covering this when it is so routine. *So what?* you're thinking. *That's what we do.*

I challenge you, though, to really think about the time, effort and cost of this sales machine against what it returns these days. The costs aren't just about the money either, with such low margins it's also a struggle in terms of pure staffing power and employee costs just to manage all these internal processes.

DISCOVERING YOUR OWN SALES MACHINE

Now I'd like you to stop and think about your own sales machine. This doesn't have to take long – just around three minutes to draw a quick sketch of what your own sales machine looks like.

 TIME OUT: YOUR SALES MACHINE

Quickly jot down what your sales machine looks like, noting about three to seven areas or 'cogs' in the machine. Start at the beginning of a campaign or procurement and end with sales messaging or advertising with customers and staff. How does this work in your retail business?

Note that you won't get the full impact of this until you actually write your own unique words and phrases from your retail environment onto a piece of paper.

Okay, now that you've written down three to seven things, how do you *feel* about those areas? What's influencing these processes? Maybe just write in the margin a word or thought about each area you've noted.

> Now, I'd like you to look over those individual bullet points and quickly jot down next to each one what it's all about, and what is really *driving* that particular process. Is it your organisation (internal), the supplier (external), or the customer (external)?

Hopefully, you've taken some time out to uncover the main cogs in your sales machine. Okay, well, I'll share first. My major cogs were something like this:

- *Supply chain:* input of product ideas, procurement, negotiations with suppliers

- *Pricing:* securing deals, further negotiations of rebates and market research of price points

- *Promotion:* giveaways, competitions, visual merchandising, promotion mechanics

- *Communications:* communicate price and product and promotions with internal staff and customers.

After looking over these areas (cogs), I thought about what areas were influencing each of them. I did this by asking myself, what was really driving these areas? Was it being influenced internally by us – the retailer? Or instead, was it an external influence by our customers, suppliers or competitors? While each area sometimes had multiple internal and external influences, if you really ask *who* has the most impact and influence, you'll get the bottom of it.

For instance, while Pricing has both a strong external and internal influence – how do you choose? One could argue that our competitors (external) have a huge influence on pricing, but at the end of the day if your competitor is selling below your cost, then as an organisation you'd either choose not to advertise that product or make sure you're making something on the deal. So, really it's the retailer that has the most influence in this area. The only deals you'll be communicating at the end of the cycle are the ones where you win.

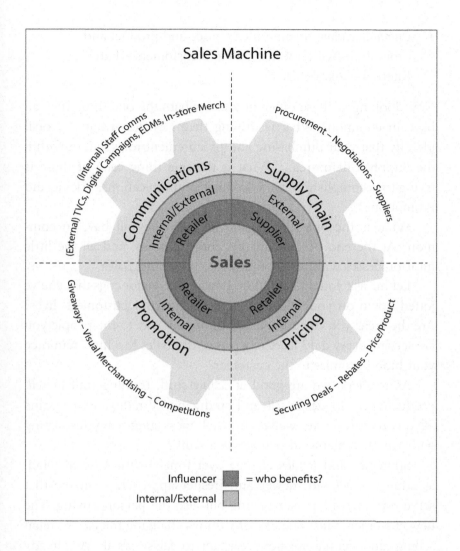

I found the following for my retail business to be true:

- *Supply chain:* input of product ideas, procurement, negotiations with suppliers – External – Supplier Driven

- *Pricing:* securing deals, further negotiations of rebates and market research of price points – Internal – Retailer Driven

- *Promotion:* giveaways, competitions, visual merchandising, promotion mechanics – Internal – Retailer Driven

- *Communications:* communicate price and product and promotions with internal staff and customers – External/ Internal – Retailer Driven

Now, looking at these different areas, what's the one thing they all have in common? What is driving them? So for instance, you'll identify that your purchasing and procurement roles will fit within the Supply Chain area... What is the one thing each of these is trying to accomplish? What's driving Communications, Pricing and Promotions?

What is the one thing that you'd say they all have in common? At the end of the day, this entire process, and all the little mini-processes within it, boil down to one thing: Sales.

Let me ask you this question: how do the major cogs that you've jotted down on your piece of paper aid in your customers' lives? Are the areas you've outlined helpful in any way to the people you are serving every day? Does *any* part of the 'Sales Machine' reinforce your brand promise to the customer?

As retailers, we are good at *selling* stuff, training staff to *sell*, producing catalogues to *sell*, and producing TV, radio and magazine adverts to *sell*. Or are we? Is this 'sell' messaging really resonating with our customers and selling more 'stuff'?

Strategies and tactics change over time. In the case of retail, as strategies get old, newer and fresher approaches emerge that serve not only the person selling but also the person buying. The new customer is just one of many things changing the face of retail selling, and people are now resistant to salesy speak. As already covered in earlier chapters, in the era of the new customer, only trusted advisors and helpful retailers have permission from the new customer to sell to them. I'm confident that if we all, you included, focus a little more on listening, building trust and helping our customers, we'll be in a much better place to start the sales conversation. What do you think?

CHANGE, CHANGE EVERYWHERE AND NOT A SALE TO SELL

8

As already mentioned in this book, retailers not focusing on selling seems counterintuitive. Our success, for the most part, is contingent on what we've been awesome at for hundreds of years – selling things. So I'm not suggesting that we forsake the art of selling; instead, what I'm suggesting is that we start looking at how much of our time and focus is put into the sales machine and how little is put into understanding, helping and being empathetic to the very customers walking through our doors.

Sure, we all have in-store and online customer surveys, but these are too often focused on the things that we are already doing and how well we're doing them. The surveys usually have little emphasis on or interest in getting our customers' input or opinions on

> The secret of change is to focus all of your energy, not on fighting the old, but on building the new.
>
> *Dan Millman*

the things that matter to them. At face value at least, our attention seems to be more focused on suppliers and their products than the very people shopping in our stores. Now, I'm not sure what your reaction to the sales machine is, but I remember thinking it was anything but customer-centric.

At the very heart of being more customer-centric is an absolute understanding of the problems our customers face and how we – as retailers – can come to the party and rescue them. If we are sports or fitness retailers, we should be inspiring our customers to get out on the weekend, or helping them find their perfect fit for active wear or footwear. We should be educating them in-store and gathering up our like-minded customers to help them along their journeys.

While our sole purpose is to provide products and services to our customers, are we really using the right strategy structure and the right approach to reach the new customer?

DIGGING DEEPER INTO THE HEART OF THE PROBLEM

Have a look back at the cogs in the sales machine I outlined in chapter 7. Note how heavily dependent these cogs were on procuring from suppliers. Stock buyers were following a very prescriptive method of being led by suppliers and only purchasing products that had the highest sell-through rates – which makes sense. What retailer would want products that don't sell well? However, none of this takes into consideration what the customer is missing out on – what's in it for them? Sure, we've well and truly covered ourselves in this sales machine. We've optimised each process to make sure we squeeze every bit of profit out. What about customers' interest and their newfound appreciation for all-out experience, however? Such a prescriptive process leaves little room for all the emotional discovery of retail – which is what customers are referring to when they talk about 'retail therapy' and the fun of shopping.

Our purchasers run sales data through their fancy-dancy buying programs, and these programs spit out what sells the best. Since people's overall preferences don't change, you find each store in your market carries the same or similar stock.

Now, Australia is one of the most franchised countries in the world and has only a small handful of department stores. So you can see how this repetitive process leads to a mundane and cookie-cutter retail environment. As big chains roll out the same methodology across their entire retail network, every store starts to look the same and sell the same gear. When you look at it under this light, it's not surprising that new retail brands from overseas get a boost in sales initially. Consumers rush to their stores hoping for something fun again, something exciting, and yet even our foreign competitors are applying the same principle.

Let me honestly ask you – now as a customer – where is the fun in walking into store after store of the same stuff? There's none – zilch, zippo.

So it's not that consumers have turned against us or that this new customer is impossible to satisfy. It's not that, as newspaper headlines might report, 'The era of the consumer has killed retail'. The fact of the matter is *we* are the ones killing retail. This prescriptive method of retailing, of purchasing and only thinking about ourselves and our profit is killing retail.

I know that's a bit heavy – perhaps you need a coffee, a wine or a scotch right now – but, seriously, if you really want to turn things around, you need to start by pushing back on this prescriptive process that is strangling us. We as retailers need to resist the conformity and the established processes and start focusing more on the customer in the very beginning of this process, starting with the products and how that product story can be told in-store.

THE NEW CUSTOMER AND THE OLD RETAIL MODEL

In the era of the new customer, as in chapter 1, it's been painstakingly obvious that our newfound narcissism, isolation and distrust are not responsive to being sold to. In fact, a large body of data suggests being too 'salesy' actually repels customers from you.

Please don't be ashamed of the part you might play in the 'sales machine'. While this was a huge revelation for me a number of years ago, now the sales machine is just a fact to be mindfully aware of. The machine was systemic throughout our entire organisation – our whole organisational chart, all of our positions within the company and the sole purpose of our work seemed to be contingent upon its shameful cogs!

Many refer to retail as the cutting edge of consumer insight – how could we be so blind, I thought? We deal with huge quantities of consumer data, market research, sales figures, logistics, merchandising studies and stores brimming full of live people and insights. It's like a consumer Petri dish for crying out loud.

Somehow in this new era of 'helpful marketing', retailers seemed to have missed the boat entirely. Sure, we had some sport, fashion and cooking blogs, we had helpful advice available online and with salespeople in-store but what else were we really doing for the customer?

In the famous words of my late Grandmother Nellie, I'll tell you what we were giving them: 'Diddly squat!'

REFINING THE EXPERIMENT

I realised moving beyond the sales machine was an important first strategy in my overall Retail Experiment. It was then that I started thinking about the topics and information that would be helpful to the customers I was seeing. I decided my local customers, and those of the clients I was now working with, deserved more of my attention – they deserved a lot more than 'diddly squat'.

So, I wrote an extensive list of things these customers might find helpful. The following figure shows what I initially jotted down.

I wrote down more than this – I had a pretty BIG list – but these were some things I jotted down with the idea that *if* we were able to give customers answers to these questions, not only would they visit the store to hear about it all, but it would also create a positive psychological experience – hopefully one that would build trust and loyalty.

Help for customers

- Information on how buying crappy and cheap appliances negatively impacts your back pocket as well as piling up at landfills at never seen before rates.

- 5 Meals you can make with a slow cooker this week (for winter).

- Best blenders for awesome smoothies.

- A week of smoothies – seven new innovative smoothies to get your morning started right.

- Efficiencies at home – how to leverage technology, gadgets and appliances to be more productive.

- Discover Paleo – how to start your Paleo journey.

- Connecting your Smart Home devices.

- Getting the most out of your Smart TV.

Being a big fan of Seth Godin, I was also interested in gathering 'like-minded' people together. In other words, we could start forming our own communities in-store and just see where that led.

Turns out, my assumptions were correct and our customers and my clients' customers loved our help with their problems.

 ## TIME OUT: WHAT DO YOUR CUSTOMERS NEED HELP WITH?

While it's fresh, quickly jot down a list of some really helpful things for your customers. Don't just limit yourself to linking to things you sell. Think of what your customers are like and what problems they have. How can you really genuinely help them?

Your smile is your logo, your personality is your
business card, how you leave others feeling after
an experience with you becomes your trademark.
Jay Danzie

Part IV

MOVE OVER,
ARNOLD ...
WE'RE TALKIN'
HUMANICS

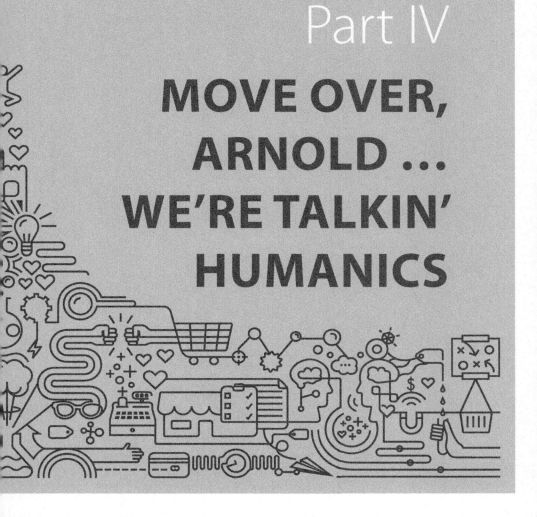

STRATEGY TWO: HUMANICS

Ya know, for some reason something about the word 'humanics' reminds me of *The Terminator*. I do love a good Arnie movie, but humanics is not quite as futuresque as it may seem. In fact, the theory is one of the oldest and most noteworthy of humankind's existence.

Humanics' broader definition is the historical study of humankind, but I'm referring directly to the human and personable elements within your retail business and, more specifically, about the in-store human elements here.

The second strategy in my overall Retail Experiment was adding a greater focus on humanics in my store. So, in the following chapters I outline in more detail exactly what this is, why it's so important for customers today, and how you can leverage this powerful tool in-store to add more personality not only from you, but from your staff and local trusted experts too.

WHAT IS HUMANICS ANYWAY?

9

So why is humanics important for retail? Consider the following:

- Psychologically, we can't relate to a business. Showing off your personality along with staff and local experts helps customers to find your store more likeable and relatable.

- Due to our own increased isolation, technology and other societal factors, we have an insatiable need for human connection.

- Now, more than ever, we are attracted to people and business personalities that are 'like us'. When we humanise our business it attracts like-minded customers, allowing us to genuinely stand out.

Find a way to be personal with your customers and connect with them on a human level.

Andrew Reid, founder of Vision Critical

- To be more relatable and 'human-like', your marketing, communications and content must use simple, everyday language to engage.

At the very heart of everything, your customer wants to feel like you understand them and their needs. Deep down, they just want to feel that you 'get them'.

Of course, we 'know' that a shop is a business, but giving human characteristics to your business gives people a sense of what your store stands for and, therefore, creates a more personal connection.

Another important point is that, as we found out earlier in the book, our tech-driven society is becoming increasingly isolated. So while we are all busier than ever, connecting with people who are 'like us' is more important now than it ever has been in history.

So to deeply connect with fellow humans and understand them, you must be comfortable with allowing your customers to see and experience your personality. Rather than just showing off your products and your branding, think of *who* you would resonate most with. Are you fighting for the rights of animals or an environmental warrior? Do you have a playful or silly side?

Our goal in humanics is to make the in-store ecosystem really welcoming and inspiring and to create a trustworthy place to visit by personifying the store in consistent ways. And we're not making these changes just for the sales machine or for shopping's sake, but for learning and entertaining, or being inspired to make changes in someone's life.

LET'S TALK AVATARS AND HUMANS, LET'S TALK LISA

Let's say you're a sports and fitness retailer, you carry all kinds of gear and have a blog to connect and reach out to your customers, as well as in-store events.

Now, let's just think for a minute about 'Lisa', your potential customer Lisa is a 37-year-old working mum with two kids. She likes running, lifting weights and is a weekend warrior who occasionally likes to hike. Now imagine that you want to connect with Lisa and help her. So you decide to get a fitness guru, 'Beck', in-store for an event. Beck is the real deal: she practically lifts weights all day, eats only raw veggies and basically denies herself any type of alcohol, sweets or other fun stuff. (In essence, this would probably sum up a lot of 'fitness gurus' out there.)

Your customer, Lisa, already knows she needs to lift more weights and eat more veggies (who doesn't?), but she doesn't make her living from working out and filtering images on Instagram to make her muscles gleam more. Lisa's got kids and work and limited time to squeeze her workouts in. Her problem isn't knowing what to do – her problem is finding the extra time and motivation to live healthier.

Now Lisa might attend an event with Beck in your store, where Beck covers more of the information that she's known for – high-intensity weight-lifting techniques and eating raw. But Lisa will likely leave feeling a little inadequate. To be honest, the kinds of people like Beck, who we often see on Facebook and Instagram, usually have to work out five days a week to stay in the shape they are, and this type of regime isn't possible for most people.

If, instead of booking Beck, you thought more deeply about what Lisa's *real* problems were, you might find an actual mum – someone who doesn't have a perfect body, for example, but has had some great wins with losing a significant amount of weight or fitness success with short, intense runs or 20-minute workouts and easy, no-fuss meals.

When Lisa finds someone who talks about the real-life struggles of juggling a family and keeping fit – problems just like hers – she's going to not only love that expert but also tell all her friends who are just like her. And she'll also love you, the retailer, for introducing her. And guess where she'll probably buy all her new fitness gear from? Yup, you. Again, this process is all about thinking about your customers and getting a feel for what their real, down-to-earth needs are. Meeting those needs is an excellent way to start connecting with your customers and humanising your store.

WORKING OUT YOUR STORE'S 'HUMAN' TRAITS

Another simple exercise to get you thinking about humanising your retail business is to decide 'who' and 'what' type of human traits best represent your store. Sounds easy, right? While it may be daunting to put yourself and your personality out there, you are probably the best person for the job. You know your business inside and out and, even if you are part of a large corporate, buying group or franchise, marketing cannot deny the power of humanising their brand.

As covered in chapter 1, and beginning with the success of our race, human connection is deeply rooted in our DNA. In fact, our innate biology craves human interaction – we just can't help ourselves. Our ancestors' very lives depended on connection with others within their tribes. The most influential people in the tribes, of course, were leaders who learned how to read and understand verbal and nonverbal behaviour.

Thousands of years later, even the most clueless of us can understand some basic clues when people are not interested in what we say or are angered or scared – without them having to mutter a word. These are the non-verbal communication clues we use, but retailers have their own language that customers pick up on too.

As already discussed, in the early days of online shopping and the growth of new retail technology, retailers were focused on and almost obsessed by this technology, thinking it was the 'golden ticket' to our problems. As we collect and input data and crunch the numbers, smart retailers recognise that the beauty of technology is that it enables us to leverage the humans we have.

However, this data is too often collected and housed on fragmented and dated systems that don't even talk to one another. And as retailers become busier and busier trying to solve the demands of the omnichannel experience with the same antiquated and disjointed systems, we move further and further away from serving and putting our customers front and centre.

Now think about your customers in this context. As we move to more complex economies as we are today, our customers are moving away from digital experiences and toward the most expensive, meaningful and experiential of all: the human-to-human experience.

If you are a retailer with an actual showroom, stop for a moment and recognise the amazing advantage you have over your online-only competitors. As bricks-and-mortar retailers, we've always had this luxury at our fingertips, yet rarely seem to appreciate it.

While digital is absolutely important in retail, especially since (as noted in chapter 2) the majority of our shoppers are researching online before even entering our stores, we need to appreciate and understand that our ability to add value, relevance and educational information – through *humans* – is the ultimate experience of all.

Humans have the ability to have deeper and more meaningful relationships with other humans – that is just how we are made. Online chat boxes are not the same as seeing someone's face and speaking with them. Online checkouts can't settle the nerves about a large purchase by allowing customers to feel a heavy or quality item. They might get a message from a chat bot asking if they can help, but it won't reaffirm the customer's decision that they made the right choice like another human being.

Online-only competitors are banking on the idea that your in-store experience isn't remarkable or leveraged. So please, leverage your physical store and use it to your advantage by humanising it.

HUMANISING YOUR STORE

I want you to take a leap of faith and draw on your own personality – regardless of how uncomfortable it might feel. If you asked ten friends about your two most prevalent characteristics, what would they say? Are you a bit nerdy, the 'class clown', a foodie, a listener, self-confident or enthusiastic? Do you love movies or are you more of the outdoorsy type? Take some time now to work out your own human traits.

 ## TIME OUT: YOUR PERSONALITY AND TRAITS

Here are a few ways to really find out what your prevalent characteristics and traits are and how they can be applied to your store:

1   Send out an email or a text message to at least ten friends, family members or workmates (more is always better). Ask them to help you identify your two most prevalent characteristics – what do they think of when they think of you?

2   Write down the top three most common responses.

3   Set your phone timer for 15 minutes and then brainstorm several ways in which the retail business you own or manage could benefit from your personal traits.

4   Next, write out a list of interests that you and your customers might have in common. Let's say you are a bit of a foodie or wine drinker or a listener – do you think any of your customers would be interested in that? Based on your retail business, what you are selling? Do you see any further synergies with products or services you have?

5   Now, out of these synergies, what types of characteristics, human traits and events do you think can benefit your customers? Is there a yearly cause or event you could really see yourself championing?

Note: It is super-critical to get feedback and insights from people outside of the organisation you own or work for. The business side of things cannot always 'think' like a human, so get that human aspect back into the equation.

Take the time to delve into activities you love and feel passionate about. These passions and the activities that come from them will allow your local customers to understand you and be more absorbed by your business, because they can see the person there, not just a national brand or logo.

So, now you know – humanics is important because it humanises your retail business and makes it easier for people to like and shop with you. And it helps us understand our customers better too.

DR GOOGLE VERSUS ACTUAL EXPERTS

10

One of my favourite forms of procrastination is YouTube, and I love the TED Talk with Tim Urban on the art of procrastination (titled 'Inside the mind of a master procrastinator' – maybe you've seen it?). I love the part where he talks about doing research (which is why I'm bringing this up in the first place), and he somehow finds himself scrolling down Google Earth on the coast of India, because he wants to learn more about India (of course, while researching the art of procrastination).

I was desperate to open this chapter with some history on the term 'Dr Google', so naturally, I turned to Google for my research, quickly entering 'first use of the term Dr Google'. Hmmmmm, not an impressive amount of information there. Soon I came across the

These days, people want to learn before they buy, be educated instead of pitched.

Brian Clark, Copyblogger founder

entire history of Google, written by Google. (You can access this history at www.google.com/about/company/history if you're after some insightful reading. Perhaps it's just my own justification for wasting so much time, but, hey – maybe you have mark-downs on your aged stock or merchandise or some other thankless and profit/soul-destroying task you should be doing. So there you go, Christmas has come early – 22 years of Google history for your reading pleasure.)

Needless to say after trawling through all that history and several newspaper stories on Dr Google I still don't have an answer of when the Dr Google term was officially first used. If you find it, please let me know for my next edition. But it is a 'thing', I swear!

FINALLY, MORE ON DR GOOGLE

So, after that longish introduction, I'll start off more simply: quite a number of years ago now, a phrase was born that was to become highly used in popular culture. This phrase was 'Dr Google'. For those who have been living under a rock, the phrase was used initially for those with physical or medical ailments who chose to seek out what was wrong by first checking their symptoms on Google. Nowadays, though, I feel it has a bit broader meaning (well, at least in my group of friends). Basically, 'checking with Dr Google' means, whatever subject you're looking for help with – whether that be to sell better, sleep better or lower your cholesterol – you can simply Google it.

What this means, of course, is that people no longer need experts or even doctors, right? Of course not – in fact, as I was already discovering through my Retail Experiment, we are now seeking real-life experts more often to share the how-tos of our problems. They can present to us directly and share their actual stories and wisdom of what they did – and what worked and what to look out for.

THE POWER OF CONNECTING WITH ACTUAL EXPERTS

Soon after starting Retail Rockstars, and as I continued to conduct my research, I found myself in a large auditorium in Brisbane. I had been invited by a friend to an entrepreneurial talk where several experts were presenting within their own very different areas of expertise, covering the topics Profile, Pitch, Publish, Products and Partnerships.

As the doors opened, we were ushered in like little sheep, all wondering what amazing things we could learn. I was excited and extremely interested in what they had to say. As a very fit-looking bloke took the stage, I heard a guy next to me say, 'Oh this guy is really good.' I immediately caught myself thinking, *Why on earth would he come again, if he'd already heard what this dude, who sounds very much like Arnold Schwarzenegger, had to say?* And I wasn't just interested in the answer because of this man's comment. I had noticed a few of our retail customers had come back for the same events on different occasions.

Of course, as the talks went on – for maybe four hours or so – I started to understand why the man had come back. The talks were really interesting, but I was still a bit curious as to the motivation behind seeing the same person present the same content.

After the presenters finished, we were invited for a bit of networking in the foyer, where I found myself still inquisitive as to why this guy (who I later found out was named Tom) came back again. I thought if I could find him, I'd ask him some more in-depth questions to better understand his motivations for returning.

As I scanned the crowd looking for Tom – okay, yes, I was stalking him at this stage – I finally located him somewhat off in the distance, near the drinks area. As I was walking towards him, the 'Arnold Schwarzenegger' presenter (yes, the one Tom had said was really good) came right between the two of us and started talking to Tom. Initially, I felt a bit strange, as if I was eavesdropping in on their conversation, but pushed past that and continued to wait as they both made eye contact with me and sort of shared the conversation. It was evident that Tom had some questions and he was using his time wisely with this expert. With that short interchange, Tom, whom I was really standing there waiting for, thanked the gentleman, turned and walked away.

Without Tom there, the speaker quickly looked at me, introduced himself and asked, 'How are you and what do you do?' I was a bit caught up in the moment and introduced myself politely but quickly retorted, 'I'm so sorry but I really need to ask that other guy something.' I felt a little disrespectful for having had the opportunity to talk to this amazing man but deciding instead to chase down a total stranger. But, that's what I did, and I took off practically running across the room to catch up with him. 'Hey', I said, not knowing his name and being surrounded by people whose names could also be 'Hey'.

Finally, he turned around, and I proceeded to tell him how I had overheard his comment about seeing the presenter before, and that I wondered if he'd come to this same event before, or to another one. He then explained that he had seen the presenter nearly eight months prior at the same event in a different city, but at the time was in the midst of selling his old business to concentrate on a new exciting startup. He went on to tell me that attending the first event gave him some great ideas that he was implementing, part of which the gentleman on stage had provoked. He was now in a much different place than he had been in eight months ago, so he wanted to listen again to the presenters and possibly sign up for their 42-week personal business program.

Well, my brain was spinning with interesting ideas and insights into what was happening inside my own store and in my clients' stores. I knew the in-store events and experiences were important and that they were definitely building advocates and trust. I also knew attendees' experiences differed from person to person, but, I hadn't quite connected the dots of how the same person could get a different experience each time depending on what was going on in their life. Now, this may seem to you like a 'D'oh!' moment, but I feel it's worth explaining in further detail.

Of course, an experience is different from person to person, because everyone will experience it in a slightly different way. The realisation I gained from Tom, however, was the very thing that would add a bit of pixie dust magic to my Retail Experiment.

As we discussed his situation, it became clear to me that he wasn't really here for the program per se; instead, he was considering buying into the program for this one expert. He wanted more of this expert and felt somehow connected to him, even though this particular occasion was the first time he'd actually spoken to him. Tom was a bundle of excitement afterwards – it was as if he'd just met Prince Charles and he was having him over for tea.

I could understand completely, however. From a psychological standpoint, Tom had associated positive change with the expert. After all, the statements and insights the speaker had shared were what sparked his own thinking and exciting new business venture. I could also see he was reciprocating his appreciation by joining this business program – which, I might add, was quite a financial investment as well as a year-long obligation. Hmmm, interesting.

This kind of commitment, of course, is not uncommon in retail – think of the time when you bought an item that really helped you in your life. Maybe it was your first MacBook or some item that had a special association with success (or even what some may call luck). And no doubt the emotion you attached to this item carried through to looking favourably on the product, the brand or the place where you bought it from.

MY EXPERIENCE WITH A BIKE SHOP

Let me tell you about an item that I was emotionally connected to, and the connection that then developed. Many years ago now, while still living in Chicago, I bought a road bike. I started riding it and was really enjoying longer and longer rides. Several of my colleagues at Maytag were into riding as well and, soon after discussing our love of the open road, we decided to enter a Maytag International team in a 550-mile (about 890-kilometre) bike ride across the Midwest for charity.

It was a wonderful adventure, our company was really behind us, and our team trained and rode together – including several people who joined later who had never even owned a bike. But we all crossed the finish line together. It was an incredible year and achievement, and a very cherished memory for me.

And it all started with my local bike shop – Village Cycle. Now, of course, the bike shop didn't really have much at all to do with my team's achievements – except that they had a flyer up in the store about the charitable ride. Then, when we finally decided to get a team together, they also held a small workshop for us on aspects like how to change a flat tire and how to adjust our brakes on the road, and showed us a couple tools that would be handy to have. Later, when those other people came on board who didn't own bikes, where do you think they bought them from? You got it – Village Cycle. And where do you think we all had our bikes serviced at, and bought our sexy Lycra shorts and jerseys and shoes from too? And it didn't stop there. In those days I didn't have children, but several of our riders were parents, and guess where they bought their kids bikes from? Yes, Village Cycle.

As I said, this was a much cherished memory for me. In fact, I associated all those wonderful memories and experiences with that bike shop and with working for Maytag. I can't tell you how many people I referred to Village Cycle over the years and I myself never would have dreamed of going anywhere else for anything that had to do with bike riding.

My bike shop: more than just a place to buy stuff

As retailers, we can be so much more than just a place to buy stuff from. We need to not only be more than just the sales machine

I introduced in part III but also capitalise on the human aspects of our business, and look at what we're providing through a local and personalised lens.

But to take this idea even further, it's important to recognise that providing help and educating our customers is essential if we want to them to associate us with the value or the goodwill they received in their own personal way. Getting back to my bike store example, other members of my team had different experiences with that bike store. Some liked the store because of what I told them (advocacy), some liked the store because they were associated with giving or supporting charitable organisations, while others, like me, associated the store with reaching a wonderful personal goal.

I think you'd agree that all of these are quite different associations, and are not something that can be easily matched by competitors just down the street. Sure, another retailer might have had some of the same bikes at the same price – maybe even in some cases at a price that was a little less. But they didn't help us – Village Cycle did.

I honestly can't say they had the foresight to do this for business reasons. I think they just genuinely wanted to help us (that's how it felt anyway), and they gave us a bike technician – or expert – who showed us what to look out for and gave us lots of insider tips. From there, we learned critical information that made us feel safer and more informed, and had the potential to make us look better on the road if we broke down in front of our fellow riders. Our ability to save face when on the road for seven days straight by changing our own tyres instead of waiting for the road crew was enough of a win for me.

LETTING CUSTOMERS LEAD THE WAY

Now, getting back to the event I attended with Tom. When he finally decided he was going to fork out lots of dough for that program, he did it because he saw the value and the potential on his own terms, not on the terms someone else had come up with, and not through someone telling him what to buy, how to buy it and when and where.

It's important to point out here that, as retailers, instead of leading and telling our customers how great a product is, sometimes it's better to let them lead the way in buying it and finding it on their own. That might mean all you do is help them identify with a certain lifestyle or the feeling it brings, or spark some ideas about what their life might be like if they were to change or adopt a certain way of living.

Knowing you have some wonderful products isn't enough, but having the empathy to know what types of experts you need to help your customers solve their problems is a game-changer, and can provide an amazing advantage over your competitors.

As retailers, we have this choice every day. We can decide whether we want to sell or whether we want to help educate and inspire our customers in fresh new and exciting ways. I've found the second option not only is more rewarding but also instils life-long trust and a real sense of community within the locality you're trading in.

Unfortunately, though, having a deep commitment and empathy for your customers can't be faked. (Or perhaps fortunately for you if you manage to get it right.) If you are really in it just for the money and you don't have a genuine desire to help people, you'll miss the opportunities your customers present you. So simply reflect for a brief moment now on a retailer's ability to actually help people, rather than constantly focusing on what's in it for us.

TIME OUT: WHAT OPPORTUNITIES ARE YOUR CUSTOMERS GIVING YOU?

Some great questions to ask yourself are:

- What are the problems my customers are trying to solve? What are they trying to accomplish? Are they trying to impress their friends and family, re-live their youth, get into shape, save time or save money?

- What types of things or activities can I do with the products I sell in-store? *Tip:* Try not to rely on the simplistic ones – for example, 'I sell ovens, so therefore I should offer a cooking class'. Think specialised – pick a particular type of cooking class that people are interested in but perhaps don't know much about. Find the niche that will really strike a chord with the lifestyle or attitude of your customers.

- What is it about my premium products that makes them so special? What are the customers like who use these products? Are they health conscious? Are they busy or sports fanatics? Recognise those premium products have more profit built in and usually serve a niche market because they are more specialised in some way.

- What is the first area of interest I should focus on? If you have lots of different products, going too wide and trying to gather too many different types of people is a mistake. The magic comes in bringing the same types of passionate people together.

LOCALISATION VERSUS NATIONALISATION

11

It's true that as we've progressed through the Agrarian, Industrial and Service Ages, and now move into what is referred to as the 'experience economy', things have dramatically changed for retail. But if anyone's up for a challenge, it's you, right?

It seems like yesterday 'bigger' was definitely better and, if a cheesy phrase could be coined for retailers' recent past, it would be 'quantity over quality'. Giant warehouse retailers like Walmart, Bunnings and BCF were killin' it. Their strategy of big showrooms, fat sales volume and skinny profit was always going to be a numbers game. They grew in the market at a time when it was easy to disrupt by low price and high volume.

Back then, the term 'local' either brought to mind the comedy skits from *The League of*

> Being locally relevant has always been the core of success in retailing, going back 100 years to the town general store whose owners knew what their customers wanted, liked and would like to try.
>
> *Stephen Quinn,*
> *CMO Walmart*

Gentlemen ('This is a local shop. For local people.') or images of dusty ol' stock that no-one wanted. If you still have those images in your head, get ready for a 'localobotamy'. While our business models may still be embracing volume and larger catchment areas, smart retailers are tapping into the localisation buzz.

Don't just take my word for it, though – consumers have been shifting their thoughts onto local versus big conglomerate brands for some time now. I mention the Edelman Trust Barometer back in chapter 1. This survey has been gauging overall trust for brands, politics and retailers alike across 28 countries since 2000. According to the 2017 barometer, Edelman found that more than half of people trust small to medium, privately or family owned businesses more than those big or publicly traded businesses. Overall, they felt smaller businesses were more responsive to customers' needs, more entrepreneurial and more innovative.[1]

And this isn't the only indicator. According to Westpac's 2015 Australia Day Index, 46 per cent of Australians believe buying from local Australian businesses is the most important thing they can do for the economy.[2] It seems, however, that while we want to support local businesses, we also want variety, good pricing and a unique atmosphere.

BIG STORES GOING LOCAL

According to Rob Blatt at Momentfeed, 85 to 95 per cent of digital consumer engagement for brands happens through location-based listings and local assets and pages. So the digital marketers seem to have figured out localisation works like crazy a while ago. The human and more visceral part of retailing seem to be late adopters, but many stores are getting there, especially overseas.

US supermarkets are certainly responding to this demand around localisation and cashing in on the local and locally sourced craze. Whole Foods Market, for example, scouts food vendors in San Francisco to provide prepared foods for its 30 northern Californian stores.

Prefer the East Coast? Wegmans Food Markets, an independent grocery chain (with 92 locations) based in New York State, started operating their own experimental farm back in 2007. Here they develop and share the best organic practices with their health-conscious customers and partner-growers (who, of course, are all local). (Really puts the 'fresh food people' to shame, doesn't it?)

Further examples are pioneer retailers like Sur La Table and Williams-Sonoma, which are both running their own local educational workshops and niched cooking classes. And insightful fitness retailers like Lululemon and NY-based 'active fashion' designer Bandier have connected with their local customers by having various types of fitness classes. Bandier's classes are not free but do offer an impressive line-up of celebrity-grade instructors – if you can get in. Whereas Lululemon has a variety of local classes (in Australia and around the world), from yoga to running workshops, all held free in-store. All of their classes are under 'Community' on their website (in the Inspiration tab), because that's, in fact, what these clever retailers are doing – creating mini-local-communities of people who dig what they are saying, what they are doing and, yup, even what they are selling.

New concept stores are also going up like crazy, with major brands figuring out that big retailers and department stores just can't tell their brand story like smaller stores can. Big retailers like Target and Macy's are also cashing in on local merchandising and replenishment, among other tactics, to become part of the communities they trade in. And even websites like yelp.com.au and special categories on TripAdvisor have been developed to hone in on the movement to help you find things like 'localvore' restaurants and locally sourced foodie tours.

GOING LOCAL IN AUSTRALIA

To understand where we are in Australia, it's important to pay homage to where we've come from. As I discuss in chapter 4, as marketing dollars began to disappear from skinnier and skinnier profits, more and more national and generic type marketing was used. Head offices went into cost-cutting mode, and so they cut costs on local advertising and marketing – because it's expensive and because it didn't benefit the 'one and all' nationalised mentality. As marketing centralised so did catalogues, email and social campaigns.

We still love shopping – and a plethora of research confirms this. But, we have changed and so have our expectations. Many years ago when the first big stores opened, it was fun to go in and try to find whatever it was we were looking for, and just see all the stuff that lined rows and rows of shelves and aisles. We'd already entered the experience economy, but it was an experience in itself just being in a large store with so much to look at.

But we got used to the massive range and, as our technology-infused lives became busier and busier, what was once seen as an experience has now become a burden. Investing 10 minutes to get to the back of the store and another 20 minutes to decide on the 75 drills presented to us isn't as appealing as it once was. So retailers once again need to adapt to serve customers by narrowing their range and deepening their inventory.

The fact remains you can get on Amazon at any time, look up that drill and order online and have it in a day or so anyway. If it's just the drill you're after, no problem – you have plenty of places to turn to. If your main concern is price, stay with Amazon. Short on time or worried about stock? Turn to the physical retailer or better yet just click and collect. But if you're looking for an experience with that drill and inspiration on some DIY projects you can get started on right now with your new shiny purchase, who do you turn to?

If you asked many of the staff at retail head offices or within advisory firms, they'd tell you this 'experience' could easily be accomplished through digital – the customer would simply turn to an online search. And yes, that's a good place to start, but for unique experiences that showcase and humanise your store don't just stop at digital, think about how they can experience it first hand human-to-human inside your showroom.

Sure, the digital marketing teams were experiencing year-on-year growth through increased data on localised searches, personal buying habits and cart suggestions fuelled by algorithms. But our physical store teams didn't get to enjoy the same spoils or wins from technology. It started to seem like the 'customer experience fairy' was only allowed to visit the digital side of retail. Most of the physical stores were left out in the cold and generically pumped out like public housing in the 1970s – store after store of the 'same-ol, same-ol', lacking any personality, local relevance or in-store experience whatsoever.

Problems with bringing a national partnership to life locally

Quite a number of years ago now, I had the opportunity to work on a project with Jamie Oliver's Ministry of Food in Australia. It was exciting times – I loved cooking appliances, cooking, drinking wine while cooking and eating my cooking! Ha! So this was right up my alley.

Each store had their own Jamie Oliver branded point-of-sale merchandise, we had some blogs and recipes on our website, and stores helped to fund Jamie's Ministry of Food Trucks – which drove across Australia providing back-to-basics cooking classes to help people in lower socioeconomic areas cook meals for their families. Jamie wanted to prove it was far cheaper and quicker to cook healthy food than order takeaway, and his tour was sponsored by yours truly and about 100 other Good Guys owners across the country. And so they set off to make a change in people's perceptions and skills.

What we didn't have was a way to bring this rather expensive partnership to life in our stores. Sure it was a great coup for us as a national retail chain, but how did this partnership really help our local customers? So I set out to find a way in which I could get a little return on my investment with Jamie locally. When his yearly signature event – the 'Food Revolution' – was on, I decided to do our own thing. Staff as well as customers were involved and we created a pretty big name for ourselves locally – in fact, the success I saw at this event was a catalyst for starting my Retail Experiment in the first place.

It became evident to me that when we dared show off our store's personality – with a bit of flair, I might add – it was noticed. Not only did our community at large respond, but our existing customers wanted to be involved too. It also geed-up the staff and got them talking about cooking healthy food – and they even came up with some great ideas on their own for how to celebrate Jamie's special day. Local schools got on board, along with their parents, and we even had our in-store departments go head-to-head in a cooking competition that was judged by our local radio station and two of our prevalent newspapers.

Don't get me wrong: as I've mentioned, I've had global and national roles, and knew all too well the branding risks that can emerge when stores are allowed to just 'do their own thing'. Some structure and limitations need to be put in place, but the power of local can't be ignored.

FIND WORKAROUNDS FOR YOUR LOCAL CUSTOMERS

Customers are speaking to us through their purchasing decisions, and they are saying things like, 'We love experiences, and we still love shopping', 'We want to be part of your "club" if it represents what we're into', 'Reach out to us in a personal way, learn what we like, teach us, entertain us and show us what you stand for so we can be loyal, tell others and never leave', because remember, 'We don't like change'.

The last bit about change is really important too – rest assured, changing buying habits is no easy task. So when you've fully engaged them, won them over and they know you, it takes a lot to get them to change again – to one of your competitors, for instance.

My point is this: when customers start voting with their wallet, a smart retailer like yourself will adjust to what you see. Don't be afraid to show off your real personality locally and let people know what makes you and your staff unique.

You may not be able to get out of your large (financially) national advertising commitments (if you're part of a larger group), but it's naive to think keeping your store and advertising generic and mixing it with a little bit of personalised digital is going to make people want to shop at your specific store. Because whether you are a huge advocator of the bigger national brand picture or not, at the end of the day, you want people to shop and spend money at your store, right?

Big nationals do have larger product networks and bargaining power, but they're often disadvantaged by the nimbleness of smaller and more locally relevant stores. It's true, a smaller retail specialist has several business advantages. Understanding what they are might help you rethink some workarounds or shortfalls in your business.

Consider the following:

- Smaller retailers can access extremely affordable but powerful retailing and marketing systems. These cost a fraction of what the big guys use and pay for.

- Being nimble and small means owners have a pulse on the locals they serve – and, therefore, can create experiences that resonate deeply within their communities.

- Smaller, niched retailers control their merchandise from start to finish. They often aren't burdened with having to stock an item because their competitor does, or because head office deems they should. Their product selection is always chosen for what's best for their customers and them.

But don't fret – many of the factors outlined in the preceding points can be equally effective for larger retailers with a few workarounds.

Here are some ideas to consider if head office controls your social page:

- use your own personal social media accounts and tag in your store to promote non-national messaging

- encourage staff to use their own social accounts to promote fun stuff happening in the store

- partner with other locals who have a real social presence, like influencers and experts in your area, your shopping centre, the store next to you, or a marketing or events consultant

- bring in local experts to deliver value to your customers and utilise their social reach

- use promotional partners for giveaways.

And if head office controls your email campaigns:

- Consider using separate opt-in email lists. We used to have opt-ins at the front desk that clearly differentiated our national email list from our local email list. We found many customers wanted in on the local messages but not the national messages.

- Make use of local email databases. These are really handy for store-specific events, fundraisers and connecting with the community.

As a retailer, you need to find your own local and unique voice. In a world of commoditised products, people are seeking a sense of community, authenticity and personalisation. Given the intense competition both locally, nationally and internationally, customers are gravitating towards and gathering in places they feel most welcome.

Even if you have a significant commitment to national marketing, you still need to put something aside for local events, experts, causes and community engagement.

Here are some further ideas for bridging the localisation gap for your store:

- Local experts can inject a 'personality' into the event. This ensures you are reaching out to the right audience and creating something that really resonates with local customers.

- Local charitable causes can really connect with your community.

- If you're a franchisee or store manager, focus on at least two events a year that are important only to your store. For example:

  – a sporting event, festival or community event held in your town, suburb or city

  – a special or significant event related to your store that happens each year – such as when you opened or when you first achieved a community milestone

  – your own special mini-expo to show off your expertise, facilitators, staff or supplier expertise

  – a few classes or educational events that help your local customers in some way.

Still stuck? Send out an email or ask customers at the checkout what kinds of things they'd be interested in learning about your products. Get your staff involved and ask them to brainstorm some possible topics that they get asked about all the time.

In a nutshell, national blanketed emails, social posts and advertising are boring (zzzzz). If your head office is in Sydney but it's raining at your store in Brisbane, you are missing opportunities to comment on the weather, or offer a free coffee, umbrella or even a special deal on dryers.

Remember – local is definitely making a comeback. If you're part of a big national group, make sure you show off your local, smaller team and adapt your in-store environment as a place to gather. Don't be shy – show off your local niche and why people should shop with you. If you're big, show off your small side; if you're national, make it a point to become more local and personal.

 ## TIME OUT: LOCALISE YOUR STORE

In the same way that nationalised messaging is generic, your store can look generic too. Make sure your in-store atmosphere is locally relevant to your customers. Is a big footy game being played this week in your city? Are you supporting a local cause? Can you entertain, educate and wow your customers with some local expertise? How can you reach out to your customers and teach them, inspire them or help them in some way?

Start capturing these thoughts and ideas down today. As you get further into experiential retailing, you can start to bring these ideas to life in your own store.

Many of the truths we cling to depend greatly on our own point of view.

Obi-Wan, Return of the Jedi

Part V

SAY WHAT? SAY EXPERIENTIAL RETAILING

STRATEGY THREE: EXPERIENTIAL RETAILING

Quick, look up and have a scan around your store – at your catalogues, advertisements and point of sale. I know you're busy but have a quick walk around and look with your own customers' eyes – what do you see?

I'm not sure about your store, but in mine the focus was mainly about products. In fact, we used part of the most familiar tactic called 'features and benefits marketing' – whereby, as the title eludes, you market the features and benefits of the product to the customer in order to sway their decision-making and aid in them purchasing it.

This kind of marketing works off the premise that people will act rationally to maximise their personal best interests when making a purchase decision. In other words, people logically evaluate products for purchases based on matching needs and motivations with features and benefits that they produce.

While features and benefits advertising might be a familiar ol' friend for us retailing folks, research has proven emotions and experiences are way more influential with customers making purchasing decisions. People don't want more stuff – they want to spend their money on experiences and products that appeal to their emotions and produce strong memories. So why are retailers still primarily focusing on features and benefits in our stores, in our catalogues and on our websites? Look, I can't totally answer that, because each retailer and their history will differ, but for our organisation, it was just part of that sales machine process and mindset of, 'Sell, sell, sell'.

The chapters in part V focus on what people are looking for instead (experiences versus product) and why your brand promise to them is so important.

EXPERIENCE SHAPING OUR WORLD

12

A few years ago, our family, like many before it, made the great pilgrimage to the magical world of Disney. I'd heard that Walt Disney World was newer and more modern but still decided on the original Disneyland in California. See, I had never been to Disneyland as a child and, of course, having been in marketing and retailing for so long, I'd heard of its wonderful attention to detail. So that was it; I determined I wanted the 'Disney experience', and I wanted it to be the 'original' Disney experience too.

When my parents were kids, the world was a much different place – and they certainly never missed an opportunity to tell us about that. Both Mom and Dad would tell stories about growing up in working class America. Besides the obvious stories of walking to

Experience is the hardest kind of teacher. It gives you the test first and the lesson afterward.

Unknown

school uphill both ways – which I'm sure are universal no matter what country you're raised in – they spoke about Christmases with little or no presents and very simple dinners, especially in times of war. And, of course, they talked about the special occasions of getting a few cents and being able to walk to the 'Candy Shop' and pick out several pieces of hard candy or lollies – which was a huge treat.

So when I was raised in the early 1970s, my parents chose to provide lots of Christmas and birthday presents and lovely meals for both my sister and me. We certainly were not short on 'stuff'. Stuff that they didn't have when they were our age, which they felt they'd missed out on. But, as most parents do, they lived vicariously through their children and decided to make up for what they didn't have. Sound familiar?

Skipping forward to today (which really is skipping forward a couple of generations) and you'll notice that we went through the 'stuff' phase when I and other Gen Xers were kids. Even the early part of Gen Ys was part of this phase. Now, two-thirds of kids between seven and thirteen would rather have technology, such as a tablet, to play with over a toy.[1]

While it's normal that we seek out those experiences that we missed out on when we were kids, it's also easy to understand our need as parents to ensure our children enjoy more experiences and less stuff. Experiences like trips to the beach or the park, bushwalks, theme parks, plays, theatre and holidays away together.

MOVING THROUGH OUR HIERARCHY OF NEEDS

A well-documented reason exists for us having these preferences for experience. In 1943, psychologist Abraham Maslow presented 'A theory of human motivation'. In the shortened 'cliff notes for retailers' version, his theory is quite simple; it outlines the five levels of human needs, shown in the following figure.[2] Each level is more sophisticated than the last, starting out with our most basic needs for water, food and shelter at the very base of the pyramid. Only once each level of need is met, can we move up the hierarchy of needs.

Maslow's hierarchy of needs

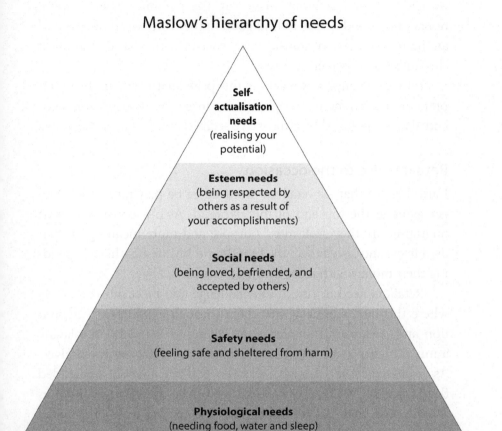

As we progress through each of Maslow's hierarchy of needs, we realise that 'stuff' isn't nearly as interesting as it used to be. After our basic needs are met, we move through to the top of the pyramid, through meeting our needs for safety, social interaction and esteem from others, up to the pinnacle which Maslow notes as 'desiring self-actualisation'. This area is really about experiences and things like expressing creativity, our quest for spiritual enlightenment and the pursuit of knowledge. Self-actualisation also encompasses the desire to give and/or positively transform our society.

As you look at your Instagram or Facebook feed, it's easy to recognise those operating further up the pyramid. Their inspirational quotes and quests to find good in the world or to rid it of evil are their own ways of transforming society – or what they think it should be transformed to anyway.

Further examples of reaching this peak are the rise in the entrepreneurial movement, the popularity in social change campaigns and also the political hiccups we've seen recently all over the globe.

Retailers rise to the occasion

I also believe that, as retailers, we need to be playing a much bigger game at the top end of this pyramid. As our consumers start migrating up, they seek more purpose and more meaning in their own lives, and also expect the brands and businesses they're spending their money with to be playing there too.

Retailers need to rise to the challenge and meet our customers where they are. Connect with them through experiences, inspiration and, yes, even transformation. Plenty of retailers are playing a much bigger game and helping to transform society themselves. As discussed earlier, though, wherever you play must be embedded deep into the DNA of your store. It must be something you yourself are passionate about. Something you seek to tease out in staff through interviews.

Successful retailers like TOMS® Shoes, Nike Stores, Whole Foods and The Body Shop are just a few who not only have amazing and humanistic retail models but also deeply connect with their transformational customers.

OH, HOW WE'VE CHANGED

When my son Harrison was five years old, we visited family in America during the school holidays after his first term of school.

Now, on the morning of the holidays following his second term of school, we were all set for a pause to the hectic schedule of school mornings – when the little guy busted into our room at around 5.30 am, excited and full of purpose. He ran to my side of the bed, slightly out of breath, and, as my eyes cracked open, he yelled out, 'Okay, I'm all packed and ready to go!' Confused and groggy, I inquired what it was that he was packed for. He replied, in his most matter of fact voice, 'It's school holidays, and I've packed my backpack to go to another country!' Even in our dazed state, it was hard not to giggle at the excitement and adventure on his little face.

As I looked at his cute, innocent face and smiled, I suddenly felt disappointed for the little guy. So I carefully delivered the news that we were home for these school holidays. Naturally, I've shared this story hundreds of times with family and friends. It's a story of absolute innocence and a real sign of the times we live in.

Going back just one generation, very few children were fortunate enough to have even travelled overseas at all, and it would have been inconceivable to think of a five-year-old catching the travel bug.

But this is where we find ourselves – as families, as parents and as retailers. Think about it: our retail customers are no different from my story. And this applies whether you are retailing at the top end of town with luxury goods or you're in the discount industry. Most people, to some extent, have experienced a major shift in lifestyle. This means expectations of retailing are now on a whole new playing field. The vast majority of customers in Australia, the UK, the US and – well, let's say most of the other affluent countries – have been migrating to the very top of Maslow's pyramid.

As we move up the pyramid to 'self-actualisation' we find ourselves squarely in the throes of experiences and transformations. Customers now weigh up the benefits of yet another purchase of 'stuff' versus an experience or a meaningful trip that is remembered, boasted of on social media and talked about for years. It's not really that hard of a choice is it? Do I want a new couch or do I want to save up for a trip to India?! In fact, you could go as far as I did and stipulate I want not only an experience but also the 'original Disney experience'.

I've mentioned *The Experience Economy* by B Joseph Pine II and James H Gilmore earlier in this book and if you haven't read it, you really should – it's a wonderful and enlightening book about our pilgrimage from the industrial revolution through to where we are today in the 'experience economy'. It's basically the economic equivalent to Maslow's more personal and motivational reasons for becoming more sophisticated so to speak.

Released in 1999, *The Experience Economy* was truly revolutionary and predicts the many types of businesses that would not survive in this new experience economy with infallible accuracy. It also outlines the economic eras the western world has gone through, from focusing on commodities through to goods and services, and then experiences and transformations. Pine and Gilmore expand on these eras as follows:

- *Commodities:* This is the Agrarian economy, where the focus is on extracting natural goods and supplying them in bulk. The seller is the trader, the buyer is the market and demand is determined by the characteristics of the commodities.

- *Goods:* This is the Industrial economy, where the focus is on making standardised products. The seller is the manufacturer, the buyer is the customer and demand is determined by the features of the goods.

- *Services:* Now we get to the Service economy, where the focus is on delivering customised services on demand. The seller is the provider, the buyer is the client and demand is determined by the benefits of the service.

- *Experiences:* The Experience economy is all about offering memorable and personal experiences over a duration of time. The seller is the stager, the buyer is the guest and demand is determined by the sensations created by the experience.

- *Transformations:* Finally, Pine and Gilmore's Transformation economy is focused on effectual and individual transformations sustained through time. The seller is the elicitor, the buyer is the aspirant and demand is determined by the traits of the transformation.

Pine and Gilmore emphasise that a focus on experiences and transformations needs a much more personal and individual approach from retailers and businesses.

Take, for instance, the classic example of the coffee bean presented by Pine and Gilmore. The coffee bean itself is a true 'commodity', and so fits nicely into the Agrarian economy. In Pine and Gilmore's example, Agrarian companies that harvest the bean or trade it, receive a little more than 75 cents per pound – that is, roughly about 1 to 2 cents a cup.

However, moving into the second economic offering – Industrial – a manufacturer roasts, grinds, packages and sells those same beans into a grocery store, turning them into a 'good', and the price to a consumer jumps to between 5 and 25 cents a cup (depending on brand and size). (Again, these prices are from Pine and Gilmore.)

Taking that a further step – into the service economy – a business such as a cafe will then brew the ground beans in, say, a large coffee urn, charging people for the coffee but allowing them to help themselves to refills. The price for the coffee may then jump to around a dollar or so per cup.

However, serve that coffee in a specialised cafe – say, a Gloria Jeans or Starbucks, or any of the speciality coffee places in any capital city in Australia – where the ordering and the crafting of the coffee is performed by experienced baristas to the individual's liking, and that further creates a heightened ambience or sense of experience. And customers gladly pay $4 to $6 per cup. This final step takes the coffee in one cup – valued at 1 cent – and transforms it into up to a $6 little cup of value. Now, I know you've got many other costs in that cup, including staff, rent and other ingredients such as milk, but you can still see the coffee goes through a massive mark-up, all based on where and to whom it is sold. I'm not sure about you, but I'd be happy if I received only one sixth of the profit coffee can provide in my retail store.

Given the above information and how long cafes have been playing in the experiential arena, it's surprising to me that we super-clever retailers have taken so long to come around to the notion. It's not just you – it's me, too. But now it's obvious – we retailers should have been playing the 'experience' game a long time ago.

LOGICAL VERSUS EMOTIONAL MARKETING

For some time now in-depth analysis and studies have been telling us that customers are anything but rational when it comes to what affects their purchasing decisions.

In his book *Descartes' Error*, professor of neuroscience António Damásio from the University of Southern California argues that emotion is not only important to purchasing decision-making, but also a necessary ingredient to almost all decisions.

According to Damásio, when making a decision, we affix values and emotions from previous experiences onto the options that are available to us. Then, these emotions create preferences that lead ultimately to our final decision.

In his own experiments, he studied people with severely damaged connections between the 'thinking' and the 'emotional' areas of their brains. He found these people had no problem with rationally processing information about options, but they were unable to make a decision because they lacked any 'emotional' links or sense of feeling around the options.

Now, this may not be groundbreaking to you, but my science-nerd brain geeks out at this. Essentially Damásio's research implies that humans – yes, us, everyday homo sapiens – must have an emotional link to process any type of decision. For those people with perfectly functioning 'thinking' and 'emotional' parts of the brain, this means we either gather up the emotional side as the retailer presents it to us, or we assign those emotions and values ourselves so that we can make our purchasing decision.

To put this another way, if we as retailers present only the 'thinking' or features and benefits part of a product, our customer will assign their own emotions to it anyway. Why not help them out and focus on eliciting influential or positive emotions from the get go? Especially when it's more important in the decision-making process anyway.

Plenty of work outside of Professor Damásio's also establishes how emotions are hugely influential in determining customer behaviour. When evaluating brands, for example, fMRI neuro imagery has shown that consumers primarily use emotions (personal feelings and experiences) rather than information (brand attributes, features, benefits and facts).

Emotions inspire action

Perhaps, though, the most important characteristic of emotions for retailers is that they spark customers into action. That's right – in response to an emotion, customers are compelled to do something. But you need to tap into their deep-seated emotions, desires and beliefs to spark them into action. I don't know about you, but just getting customers to take notice and maybe to take some action was good enough for me.

Effective retail marketing today is about uncovering people's emotions and desires and helping them to solve meaningful problems. It's not about tricking or manipulating people into buying more 'stuff' they don't need. It's about uncovering your customer's genuine aspirations, and then allowing them to feel the benefits of achieving these aspirations through the help of your store.

So, while logic (features and benefits) can help and should not be left out of the retail equation entirely, people rarely act by reason or logic alone. As discovered though, we've still got plenty of features and benefits marketing around the place. You need to tap into customers' deep-seated emotions, desires and beliefs to spark them into action. You need to add real genuine value, and you need to help them solve their problems in fun, educational and entertaining ways.

So, in many ways, what I'm saying here today is nothing new, and we've touched on it throughout this book. But, I'm challenging you to walk into your store with these new 'customers' eyes'. Seek out and find any emotional and engaging experiences on your showroom floor. If you think you have a plethora, great, put the book down – you've earned to right to post #retailexperienceking on social. (I'll be looking for you!) If not, keep reading and make sure you complete the following Time Out.

 TIME OUT: EMOTIONS

Here's how to start thinking about the kinds of emotions you could hope to evoke in your store:

- Block out 30 minutes to walk your sales floor tomorrow – put it in your schedule now, so you don't forget.

- Now set your phone timer to 15 minutes and start jotting down some initial ideas on emotions in your store. Taking into consideration the types of products you sell in-store, what are some strong emotions customers could have related to them? Just start randomly jotting down ideas any way they come. For example, relating to home appliances, customers could be inspired to cook healthier, lose weight and exercise more. Or they could feel intrigued by technology and new products, or fear that they aren't providing the right nutrition. Focus on these fear emotions in particular – fear of ill health, fear of wasting time, fear of money problems. Also, think about the emotions connected with inclusion – customers want to fit in, be on trend and even show off to their friends.

- Now look over your extensive list of emotions, and pick out three that you feel most passionate about. Spend some time elaborating on each one. As you walk your sales floor for 30 minutes tomorrow, think about how you could evoke these emotions in-store.

DISCOVERING THE STEPS IN YOUR CUSTOMER JOURNEY

13

Now, it's all well and good to talk about experience – in fact, most people are these days. I've been to three retail conferences just in the last six months, and it seems 'customer experience' is the hot new topic.

I've been 'going on' about retail experience for well over five years now, so it's lovely to see my hypothesis (told you I was a science nerd) being discussed and bantered about. But while I'm loving the enthusiasm around experience in retail lately, what I don't appreciate is the supposed mysteriousness of it. To date, I feel these ideas are treated a bit like the ol' 'smoke and mirrors' days in advertising, whereby only a few gifted grand poobahs knew the secrets.

Let me give you an example. Earlier this year, I attended a retail conference and, for

> The chance to make a memory is the essence of brand marketing.
>
> *Steve Jobs*

the first time in years, about 50 per cent of the keynote speakers spoke about customer experience. What was slightly annoying (and, I suppose, fortunate for me) is that many of the 'experts' who talked about the importance of customer experience had little or no examples to support their claims. And then the big retailers who did dare share had campaigns that were so complex and expensive they were irrelevant to small retailers. It seemed to be more of a dog and pony show than a genuine desire to help struggling retailers.

As with any new strategies, I suspect consultants and experts get onto a good thing and then ruin it by making the interested people believe they must hire a really expensive consultant or their entire idea will blow up in their face. I'm here to tell you, though, that rather than investing in a 'bigger than Ben Hur' campaign that costs millions, you can work within your own branding and personal interests to create something meaningful to your local customers.

Within the four walls of our retail stores, we have complete control over the experiences our customers have, so why not engineer experiences that are inspirational, meaningful and memorable to our special people – our local customers?

DEVELOPING AND THEN BUILDING ON YOUR BRAND PROMISE

Not long ago, I listened to a webinar on retail customer experience (CX) where the presenter stated,

About the worst thing you can do is to spend bucketloads on branding and advertising to drive people into your stores and then leave it all up to a $20-an-hour employee to pull off your entire brand promise.

And he's not wrong. While your team is critically important, there must be more than just a 'staff experience' waiting for customers as they enter your store.

As I've discussed through this book, consumer expectations and behaviour are rapidly changing. In particular, what triggers our purchasing decisions, as well as what drives us away, have changed dramatically. Retailers winning today are super-diligent about infusing their own brand essence or promise into customers as they walk inside their stores.

It's important also to know that we are on the cusp of a retail revival, where customers, retailers and experts will be paying a lot more attention to the physical side of retail. As online sales begin to slow down (from previous double-digit growths year on year), we are now starting to see a bit more focus return to the more visceral and physical components of retail.

With this in mind, let's start thinking about your brand story and what it really means to be a customer of your store and to work there.

To get the most out of the chapter you need to allocate some time to thinking about your own unique brand promise. As we learned in part IV on humanics, people need to know the person behind your store – and what you stand for and why.

Mapping out your customer journey and assigning and reinforcing your brand promise are at the heart of your in-store customer experience. The pyramid shown on the following page illustrates how your brand promise will lay the foundation of your entire in-store experience.

The stages in developing your overall brand promise and then building on it are as follows:

- brand promise (BP)
- unique retail customer experience (RCX)
- identifying retail touchpoints (RT)
- diagnosing emotions (DE)
- developing experiments for your store (E)
- measurement (M)

Whether you are part of a franchise or large buying group, or a small boutique retailer, you will have a brand promise. If part of a larger organisation, you may already know it. If not, reach out to your marketing department to get it. If smaller and you're not sure, it's worth spending some valuable time distilling it as you go through the following sections, or hiring a professional to help you.

6 steps to building your own unique experiences

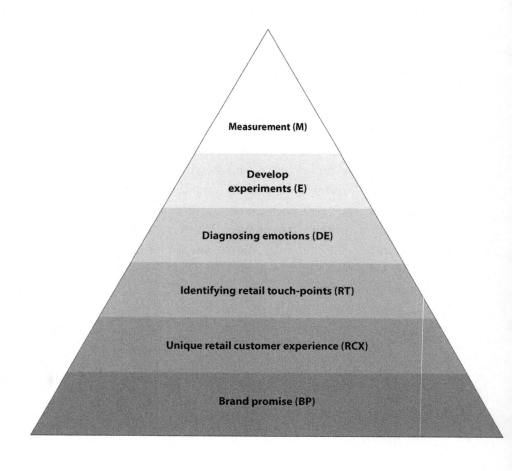

6 STEPS TO BUILDING YOUR OWN UNIQUE EXPERIENCES

Let's dig deep and start thinking about how you can build your own unique experiences in-store in the six areas of your store's pyramid – starting with your brand promise.

Step 1: Finding your brand promise

As I said, we all have a brand promise. Establishing your brand promise is all about finding your brand's meaning. Essentially, we are talking about what it is that you promise your customers. Are you inspirational, ecological, sensible or maybe fun-spirited? As you look at the examples I've provided in this section, I hope you'll get a sense of not only what the brand's promise is but also their personality.

And remember – a brand promise is an internal declaration, not an advertising tagline. The brand promise is what a company's marketing and advertising are built upon. For instance, US Target's brand promise is, 'Provide well-designed products at an economical price'. However, its advertising slogan is, 'Expect More. Pay Less'.

Nike's brand promise is, 'We understand the soul of an athlete', but its iconic slogan is, 'Just Do It'.

Some further famous retailer or iconic brand promises from past and present include:

- H&M: 'More fashion choices that are good for people, the planet and your wallet'

- Starbucks: 'To inspire and nurture the human spirit – one person, one cup and one neighborhood at a time'

- FedEx: 'Piece of mind'.

Note that brand promises are not published or talked about much publicly, so I've used a few overseas brands and retailers that have publicly disclosed them in the news or with business or advertising agencies.

In addition to the examples above, you need to consider several things when brainstorming your brand promise. I suggest while brainstorming (and after) you check your promise against these four key criteria:

1   *Make it measurable:* If you have the word 'friendly' in your brand promise, can you measure this? (Many companies can, but make sure you confirm it's possible, either now or in the near future.) Is your brand promise something your staff can pull off and understand easily, and can you make this evident when walking in-store?

2   *What does your customer really need?* How can you help your customer with something they really need? Notice I didn't say 'want'. Customers will always 'want' things – in fact, they can 'want' you straight into insolvency if you let them. You may already be doing something really well – is that fulfilling a need?

3   *Make it meaningful by delivering:* If your promise is significant to your customers and makes you different from your competitors, that's meaningful. But can you deliver it? Remember the old adage comes into play here: 'actions speak louder than words'. A brand promise is nothing if it's not followed through with action. The one thing successful retailers do well is deliver on their brand promises consistently. When you make a commitment to your customers, you must deliver, or they will leave you.

4   *It doesn't have to be forever:* Brand promises do and should change as the market changes. Take, for instance, the FedEx promise. When they first started out in the 1980s, their slogan was, 'When it absolutely, positively has to be there overnight'. One thing in business is guaranteed: if you are successful, other businesses will try to match your services, so your brand promise may change over time. For instance, in the case of FedEx, several years later new couriers had appeared and existing ones had upped their game, and delivery by

10.30 am became the norm. In many ways, FedEx lost its brand promise due to its own success. After strategising what their customers really needed, they invested millions in new technology and systems, making terminals and tracking systems available to all businesses both big and small. This helped eliminate anxiety and break down the time and entry barrier. Because their customers' needs changed, they reinvented their brand promise to, 'Peace of mind', which shifted their tagline to, 'Relax. It's FedEx'.

TIME OUT: ARTICULATE YOUR BRAND PROMISE

If you don't already know what your brand promise is, take the time to track it down. If you're part of a larger organisation, call your marketing department. If you're an independent retailer, just jot down your best thinking at the moment – it doesn't have to be perfect, the idea is to get you thinking about your brand promise and acting.

So, what's your best thinking right now? What is your brand promise?

Step 2: Finding your unique retail customer experience

Next, as you look over your brand promise, what do you think? Does your promise include emotion or inspiration? When looking to uncover your unique retail customer experience, we are defining how your retail brand manifests itself – what uniqueness do you bring? Could some pointer words lead to an emotional connection? What are they?

Here's another example – this time from Southwest Airlines – of how a brand promise can translate into experience:

- *Brand promise:* Friendly, reliable, low-cost air travel.

- *Unique experience:* Surprising, delightful, personality-driven air travel.

While Southwest's internal promise is clear – they want to be known as friendly – they also want their name associated with reliability, and they aren't aiming at luxury travel but low-cost travel. So, they've looked at those action words of 'friendly' and 'reliable' and want to add how these are experienced for external use – articulated through the 'unique experience' they offer. Although they are still adjectives, 'surprising' and 'delightful' are much more evocative words than 'friendly' and 'reliable'. Focusing only on 'low-cost travel', on the other hand, means they don't have lots of room for surprising people with luxurious things or services; however, they realised their staff (if hired properly) could inject their own personality into air travel. If you've ever travelled with Southwest you know this personality is there – each announcement for example, rather than being the boring 'robot' version, is personalised and unique. This is always delightful and many times surprising too. This is similar to approach Virgin Australia took when entering the low-cost air travel market in Australia.

So make your unique retail customer experience emotional and memorable. The best brands and retailers capture emotions and/or senses, which fires up certain parts of our brains, making us remember better. Apple, for instance, is great at forging intimate connections. These emotions and senses are felt while shopping, discovering, owning and using Apple products.

While reviewing your brand promise, look for ways to use more emotional or evocative words that capture your own unique store experience. Is it fun, is it funky, is it for the old or young, playful or a little serious?

TIME OUT: CAPTURE YOUR UNIQUE STORE EXPERIENCE

If you are really good at a particular thing, how could that make someone *feel* more? Glean what you can from the Southwest example in this section, and note that their brand promise wasn't word-smithed to death. As they applied the promise to the 'experience' of this promise, the words used became more evocative of emotion.

So build from your brand promise, but make the way this is experienced more emotional. Involve the senses or create a visual that's in-line with what you guys are all about or how you want to make it even better. This is also an excellent opportunity to look, for instance, at your corporate brand promise (if you're part of larger group) and inject some of your own unique (local) experience into it. Base this off what you discovered in part IV on humanics.

Step 3: Identifying your in-store retail touch-points

Next let's explore your retail touch-points and, for this exercise, let's just focus on your in-store touch-points. Touch-points allow your customers to have an 'experience' every time they 'touch' various parts of your business. These are the actual moments when you as a retailer interact with your customer, so think of common areas like the spaces where customers are facing staff inside your store. Also consider people who aren't staff or customers who are in your store, like suppliers, demonstrators and consignment staff.

To help you start thinking about your store's touch-points, here are the seven areas I listed for my store (you may have more or fewer):

- cashiers

- reception

- sales teams

- warehouse

- warranty or customer service

- security

- click and collect (pick up in-store for online sales).

TIME OUT: YOUR IN-STORE TOUCH-POINTS

Brainstorm all of the touch-points for your store. Just make a simple list, as I did, entering each type of staff who interact with customers, both face to face and over the phone. Enter your best thinking – it doesn't have to be perfect or all-inclusive, just quickly jot down the areas where customers 'touch' your business.

Step 4: Diagnosing emotions

While many retailers hire agencies to distil their brand promise and implement other important metrics for communicating with customers, many times super-important details like identifying specific emotions for each touch-point can be glossed over. I believe the best people for investigating emotions are you and your staff. Even with the help of market researchers, agencies don't get the real customer sentiment like you and your staff can.

For each touch-point that you've identified in the previous step, think of at least two corresponding emotions – you might have more. Think in terms of positive and negative emotions that are associated with that touch-point, and try to have at least one negative and one positive for each. When considering what could be positive or negative, consider the following:

1   Positive emotions produce gratitude, delight or inspiration for that touch-point – for example, the in-store register or payment area could be surprisingly efficient or personalised and funny with enjoyable staff interaction.

2   Negative emotion produces friction, frustration and disappointment – for example, the register or payment area could be subject to many interruptions and staffed with slow or rude staff.

Here are the positive and negative emotions I noted for two of our seven in-store touch-points:

1 Cashiers:

- *Positive:* Cheerful and funny (staff encouraged to be silly and have fun).
- *Negative:* Frustration (when there's a wait, systems not great, take longer than should sometimes).

2 Warehouse:

- *Positive:* Grateful (for help with lifting and being careful with new products).
- *Negative:* Frustration (sometimes people have to wait).

 ## TIME OUT: TEST THE EMOTIONS OF YOUR TOUCH-POINTS

This exercise comes in two parts. First, next to each touch-point, write the corresponding negative and positive emotions. Keep in mind these emotions should be as 'real' as possible and diagnose how they are right now (we will work on future upgrades later). Using actual praises or complaints received makes it even more realistic. Once finished above, move onto the next part.

Now, *stretch* it: look at your list and compare these emotions with your brand promise. What do you see?

For instance, when I did this exercise, I realised one of our key words in our unique customer experience was 'personalised' and another was 'super-helpful'. When I reviewed all of our existing touch-points, however, I realised we didn't really have the capacity, salesperson-wise, to be 'super-helpful' on the sales floor. After all, most of the customers were pretty clued up on the products already from visiting our website prior.

So we decided that in addition to going out of the way when we could on the floor (which I'll expand on in the following section), we'd also find experts on various topics and have experiences and workshops to tackle the 'super-helpful' part of the promise.

Step 5: Developing experiments

Based on the touch-points you have identified and evaluating the negative and positive emotions of each touch-point, can you identify some opportunities, ideas or experiments where you can make improvements? It may be the case that you need to add another touch-point in – for example, like in the example in the previous section where we invited experts in to do workshops. However, the improvement could be as simple as adding an additional responsibility or checklist to an existing touch-point.

For instance, we had several complaints from customers about getting home after buying a printer and being frustrated that they couldn't even use the machine because they didn't have the right cables. The manufacturers of printers stopped including connecting cables with the printers to reduce the recommended retail price point, but this was a major source of pain for our customers. So we developed checklists for products that we knew had similar issues. Each time a customer bought these 'flagged' items, the sales staff had to check whether the customer had everything required for set up.

Most likely you can quickly fix some emotions tied up with touch-points right within your own store. Other times, however, you'll need to look elsewhere – perhaps to other people or potentially adding in additional touch-points to reduce the friction or even to add more joy to something that is already working.

What's important to remember here is this is your store, and you and your staff viewing these ideas and opportunities as experiments removes the 'procrastination by perfection' virus. Once we start viewing our stores as evolutions in retail rather than processes that cannot be changed, we can start making more and more incremental and meaningful changes for our customers.

TIME OUT: REVERSING NEGATIVE EMOTIONS, CAPITALISING ON POSITIVE ONES

Start out by first analysing the negative emotions for each touch-point. What are some ways you can make the customer experience better, with less friction?

Now look at the positive emotions for each touch-point. How could you really capitalise these emotions or formalise the process or service to make them more consistent?

Quickly jot down your ideas for improvement and how you might develop small experiments throughout your store, and pick your top three.

Step 6: Measurement

Like anything in business, what gets measured gets improved – and your retail customer experience is no different. In fact, in many ways, the most important steps are developing the experiments and measuring them. While it may be easy to get entrenched in the importance of your brand promise or your unique retail experience, it's the mind shift from all-out to all-in that can really make the difference. That is, rather than thinking of your retail business as an all-out process with big rollout campaigns, it's far more useful to explain to staff that you like to try small experiments to improve customer experience, test them and keep the good ones. This subtle shift from all-out to all-in means you're focused on coming up with ideas and experiments all the time, and it soon becomes part of your culture to experiment and also to measure whether it worked or not.

Experiences can be measured and – while many will tell you that you have to have a sophisticated system to do so – the best systems for these experiments are real live people asking real questions. Another simple option may be a free app on an iPad with three questions from Survey Monkey. By now, you will have identified your top three areas for improvement. The final part of your analysis is to measure them – and determine whether it's something you want to make a permanent change in or something that needs a bit of further work. Measurement is a pretty straightforward concept – what you are looking for is whether your experiments are resonating with your customers. Every time you introduce a new experiment, it's imperative that, before the experiment goes live or you start implementing it with customers, you have a way to measure if they liked it.

One area you should always focus on is simplification. Simplify everything in your store – from your cashiers and phones to sales staff and the warehouse. Remember, if it's not simple, they are not buying.

TIME OUT: MEASURING YOUR FOCUS AREAS

Quickly look at your top three ideas for experiential retailing from the preceding step. Now next to each idea or experiment write out a way to measure it. Again, try to simplify this area too – it might be as easy as asking customers after each checklist is delivered, or a quick four-question survey after a workshop is delivered – but it must be measured.

TIME OUT: IMPROVING FOCUS AREAS

Schedule a meeting with your managers or best staff and discuss your top three areas of focus. Gather input and ideas on how to improve these touch-points and select a date – for example, a week out from the meeting – when you'll start implementing and measuring at least one of your top three ideas.

Remember – your brand promise is *mucho importante* – or, for those not familiar with Spanglish, it's critical to your in-store experience.

Spend some time going over the 'Time out' exercises from this chapter this week, and start thinking about those super-important retail touch-points and how you can improve your customers' in-store experience. What can you do to add more emotion and lasting memories of you, your staff and your store? What will really make them remember your generosity and helpful nature? Above all, remember that the creation of these experiences is not to 'extract' revenue but rather to create 'value' for your in-store customers.

A story is a journey that moves the listener, and when the listener goes on that journey they feel different and the result is persuasion and sometimes action.

Jennifer Aaker, marketing professor at Stanford's Graduate School of Business

Part VI

RETAIL STORYTELLING AND A GOOD NARRATIVE

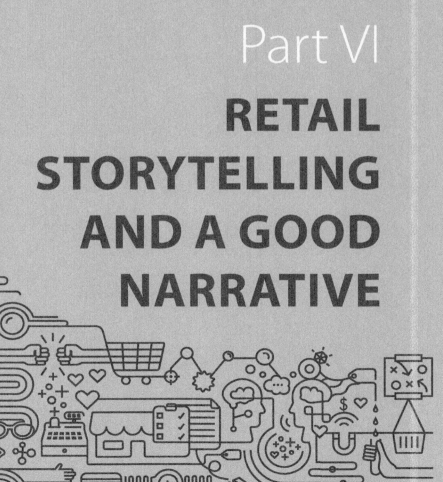

STRATEGY FOUR: RETAIL STORYTELLING

It's certainly no secret that storytelling is effective at engaging people, so it probably comes as no surprise that if we're looking to engage our customers, it's going to be a great tactic to use.

While tonnes of statistical and neuro studies support the impact of storytelling, the simpler and less formal study done by Jennifer Aaker (quoted on the previous page) sums it up best.

Aaker assigned each of her students to give a one-minute pitch. Only one in 10 students incorporated a story within his or her pitch, while others stuck to more traditional pitch elements like facts and figures.

When the professor then surprised the class and asked them to write down everything they remembered about each pitch, 5 per cent of the students were able to cite a statistic, but a massive 63 per cent remembered the stories.

So it's time to start using this power to engage your customers through powerful stories – the following chapters show you how.

THE IMPORTANCE OF RETAIL STORYTELLING

14

The internet and the publishing worlds are not short on information on storytelling – a quick check on Amazon tells me they have over 11,991 books on the subject.

And it's true that a lot of areas in business already utilise storytelling, but the top-end of town would like you to believe creative agencies are the only ones able to leverage this power. Nothing could be further from the truth, though, and retail storytelling is an imperative skill to have in your arsenal. Storytelling is an incredibly powerful and efficient way to communicate your ideas, brand, services and products. Done correctly, it can evoke a deep emotion, connect with customers and motivate people or staff to get on board with your idea or influence their decision-making process.

> If your stories are all about your products and services, that's not storytelling. It's a brochure. Give yourself permission to make the story bigger.
>
> *Jay Baer, author of* Youtility

TAKING ADVANTAGE OF RETAIL STORYTELLING

Here are some ways I used storytelling in my retail business:

- Whenever I had to make major changes to commission structures or introduce new policies or procedures, I'd use a story to explain why.

- When boring and very corporate communications came from our head office (usually in the form of 150 pages of blah-blah-blah), I'd read the communications, simplify them and create a story that made (positive) sense to everyone.

- At any customer events, I'd develop a retail story that I'd share with staff, customers, media, other local business and suppliers alike.

- At appropriate times with staff, suppliers and customers, I'd share my story – how I came to Australia, how I came to own my business and my background.

- Other times, I'd share my store's story – who we were, key messages and points of difference.

- When merchandising I'd use products and other items to tell a lifestyle or brand story.

So, as you can see, I like to use stories to convey lots of complicated ideas or explain the reasons behind events or changes in retail. Anyone who knows me personally realises this is just part of my personality, but it's also something you can easily learn. I know because I've taught the skill to not only my staff but also other retailers. It seems the consensus echoes my thoughts and feelings exactly – which is that storytelling is super-easy and useful. It's easy to learn and works because it's easier for us, the tellers, to remember and easier for the people who hear it too.

In fact, our very existence in the early days of civilisation depended on our ability to tell or retell a good story. This story-telling ability would help us fight animals using techniques that had worked well for others, protect tribes from disease (and treat the disease if required), and many other important survival techniques. For a very long time, storytelling was our only way of passing along valuable information.

Indigenous cultures on every continent relied heavily on the use of storytelling. While brute strength in leaders was highly revered, strength alone was not enough to successfully lead a tribe or community. An outstanding leader could not only tell a great story but also evoke emotions and motivate their communities to rise up against predators, rival tribes and, essentially, lead their people to victory and safety.

And with all the talk about our disengaged customers in retail and attacks from global competition, storytelling is a great weapon to have in your retailing arsenal.

WHY STORYTELLING IS SO POWERFUL

Retail storytelling is super-powerful for your store, for your events and for your staff and customer engagement. Clarity is essential and putting together bite-sized chunks of useful information will help not only your employees but also your customers to retell the story for you. How good does that sound?

But rather than me labour on about how awesome it is, abundant research and science have identified the significant physical changes that occur in our brains when we move from listening to facts like features and benefits to gaining the same information within a storytelling framework.

When we listen to a PowerPoint presentation or some salesperson ramble on about features and benefits or why our retail store is better than another, certain parts of our brain get activated. Scientists call these the Wernicke's area and the Broca's area (shown in the following figure[1]). In a nutshell, the information hits the parts of our brains that process language. This is where we decode and process words into meaning.

The Wernicke's area and the Broca's area

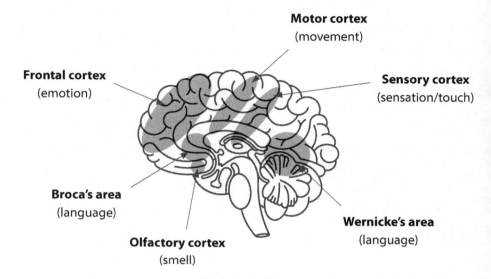

However, when we are being told an engaging story, even if we can't see the product or smell it, when we are fully immersed in a good story that references sight, emotion and movement, each area responsible for those senses lights up our brain like a Christmas tree. Even though it's just a story, we're still using the language-processing parts, but we're also using other sensory areas, almost as if we were actually experiencing the sights and sounds or the smells of the story ourselves.

This is where the magic with storytelling really happens – by involving and engaging more parts of our brains, we can have our own unique experiences and remember them more vividly.

So while you might have an in-store event which utilises story-telling, the experience is enhanced not only for the actual attendee, but also when they are retelling the stories to family or friends. The people hearing the story second-hand will actually remember and have similar experiences to the original attendees.

Please, for me, use your storytelling powers for good

Historians, religious scholars and psychologists have all studied the power of stories with the sole intent of revealing and dissecting the magical elements that move, motivate and drive people. And once you've uncovered these same elements, you have an extraordinary amount of responsibility to use these powers for good – we've seen the perils of what happens when a great storyteller like Adolf Hitler, for instance, takes the stage. As Franklin D Roosevelt said (but was more popularly paraphrased by Spider-Man's Uncle Ben) 'Great power involves great responsibility'.

Because, you see, stories are already hardwired into our DNA. Great stories, regardless of their intent, take your audience on a journey; they inform and can even shock those listening into action. But take great care when formulating a self-obsessed and untruthful story – this can do more harm than good for you and your business.

RESONATING WITH HUMANS AND HEROES

Earlier in this book we spoke about the importance of understanding humans and how our heightened emotional states, isolation and attention deficiencies all play a part in our purchasing decisions. I want to bring our personal roles to the retail forefront again here. As we move into stories and how they can help you influence customers as well as staff and suppliers, it's important to consider who your audience is.

It's pretty obvious that you'd speak to your customers differently from how you'd speak to your own staff or even a supplier, but I'm talking more specifically than that. To truly resonate with whomever your story is made for, you must try (as best as you can) to understand these three important elements about them:

- *What motivates them:* What really gets them going? Honour, money, fame? What's lacking in their lives? What do they desire most?

- *What their lifestyle or genre is:* Are they hipsters or nerds – or both? What's it like to be them and where would they hang out?

- *What they know:* What do they know already about your story or topic? Where and how do they get their 'intel'?

In addition to understanding who you're speaking with, you also need to identify who the 'hero' is in your story. To give a better idea of what I mean here, I thought I'd use two important characters from one of my all-time favourite movies – the first *Star Wars* movie, or what George Lucas famously renamed as *Star Wars: Episode IV – A New Hope.*

At the start of this movie, Luke Skywalker is young and working for his aunt and uncle on their dusty farm. He meets and then finally gives in to Obi-Wan, who is a Jedi Master, and learns the secrets of using the force by training to be a Jedi. He ends up destroying one of the enemy's major weapons and is widely accepted as the hero.

Obi-Wan, on the other hand, is a rather mysterious and wise Jedi Master. He looked over Luke while he was still a farm boy, and later gives Luke his father's lightsaber and trains him in the ways of the force, both physically and mentally, acting as his mentor. He later sacrifices himself to save the others.

Importance of the hero

Many people, whether they are in business or retail, like to see themselves as the Luke character – the hero. This is a naturally occurring phenomenon – people dream of being the centre of attention. We all aspire to be the strong hero of the story, someone who is blessed with not only skills but also a bit of luck too. It's important to understand, when you're hoping to connect and move people, that they too want to be seen as the hero.

A really good storyteller will make sure they are more like Obi-Wan – a mentor who is there to help and guide his heroes with wisdom and moral support. You'll notice that all heroes must come to their own conclusions on how they want to act – for example, whether they want to, as Luke did, take up arms and fight back as a member of the Rebel Alliance. Obi-Wan never forced Luke into action; Luke had to cross that line for himself – and so does your storytelling audience.

Notice also that Obi-Wan never talked down to Luke, or tried to make himself look the hero but is always giving insights, knowledge, skills and instilling confidence in his young protégé.

For me, this is the key to good storytelling – it's all about giving and teaching. So you want to start from a place of giving to see what insights and what knowledge you can give to your audience and provide them with enough motivation and confidence when they're hesitant or fearful.

So, first and foremost, remember that your audience – or your customers, staff and suppliers – are the heroes (or the Luke Skywalkers) in the story. You, as storyteller, are the mentor (or the Obi-Wans).

A STORY (OF COURSE!)

You've probably heard the phrase, 'Business life versus personal life' or perhaps been asked something like, 'Are you going there for business or pleasure?' That kind of separation has always really annoyed me, because it seems to assume that no person or personality exists within the business. This is counterproductive to what we're trying to achieve here. For too long retailers have been scared to show off their personalities.

A good story is a great way to mix business with personal and connect with your customers, to show off your personality, hand down some insights or value and put context around what you're trying to achieve. Let me give you an example.

About ten years ago – about the same time a high-school friend of mine was diagnosed with multiple sclerosis (MS) – I started participating in a 100-kilometre bike ride for MS called 'Brissie to the

Bay'. I coerced one of our staff to join me in my journey and got jerseys printed up. I also decided to put together a media release about our fundraising goals, a sale we'd planned where 1 per cent of sales went to our cause and how people could help by stopping by and donating.

The journalist called me and asked a whole bunch of questions, covering aspects like what my motivation for doing this was and whether I knew anyone personally who was affected by MS.

After the lovely story the journalist wrote was released, I realised it was so much better than my boring media release. It spoke about me and my friend Wendy, the sports we had played together in high school and some funny moments we'd shared (I do think I got a bit carried away with the journo on the phone). I didn't include any of this information in my media release because I didn't think anyone would care about me or my long-lost friend in America, but it turns out they did.

Lots of local people donated to our cause and, as I continued with the event each year, more and more staff would join me, as well as some local customers, and I eventually gained some corporate sponsors. And that story continued to give people a reason to join in years later, to fundraise and to help the MS Society even more.

Modifying your story for resonance

With each telling of every story, you need to find what resonates with your audience and what motivates them, along with what their knowledge and lifestyle is. This means each story is simply modified for its own audience – which is something you'd do naturally anyway in conversation. In other words, my story about the MS ride to a potential sponsor or supplier would still contain the main story about *why* we do this ride annually, but sponsors want to know what's in it for them – remember, they are the heroes here, in this case helping me raise more money for MS. So I would also include reports from the previous year's media reach, and also how we would bring more attention to their products – such as their bike GPS units.

When talking to new employees, I'd include the same main story about *why* we do the annual ride, but include how awesome they were going to feel by helping raise money, how fit they were going to be and how they'd get one day paid off work to do the ride and another day off to relax – now that's incentive!

Again, as a retail leader, you'd do this naturally in your conversations but what really takes your storytelling to the next level is when you actually sit down to plan and write out the story purposefully for each audience.

SIMPLE ARCHITECTURE OF A STORY

Retail storytelling is similar to regular storytelling in that, in its simplest form, it is a connection of cause and effect. The more simplistic your story, the more likely it is that that it will be remembered, be emotive and super-sticky – so make sure it's short (like under two minutes) and keep it punchy.

Research has revealed that our brains learn to ignore really complex or overused words and phrases, so also make sure you avoid buzz words.

In my experience with retail managers and owners, I've found the best approach is to keep the structure super-simple too. In a nutshell, the architecture of a story only has three moving parts, sometimes referred to as Acts I, II and III:

1 *Beginning, Act I:* Summary of critical parts within, establishing the problem with the way things are, a glimpse of the new idea/change/information.

2 *Middle, Act II:* Your new idea/change/information in more detail, or new way of doing things. Contrast this back to the beginning – how they differ and why.

3   *The End, Act III:* The steps that led to the conclusion and the key messages. How things will be different, and what the moral or take away is.

The following chapter expands on these storytelling ideas, with more help on how you can create your own story.

 TIME OUT: FINDING YOUR HEROES

Think about your store's customers and the types of people who visit. You might be lucky and already have a retail niche – if so, this will be even easier. Think of the different groups of people who shop with you – they might be entertainers, scholars, into health food, young mums or businesspeople. List out as many types of heroes for your store as you can think of.

Now write next to each type of hero what you think they would be interested in learning about, inspired by or keen to experience.

USING STORIES LIKE A PRO

15

While you can utilise storytelling in many areas in retail, here I'd like you to focus on the most important story first – your own. Later in the chapter, we'll quickly look at using visual storytelling through your merchandising and product placement.

YOUR OWN RETAIL STORY

If you don't have a retail story, you need one. Consider what you could include in a quick, two-minute (or less) story about *why* you and your business exist. What's your retail story?

If you do have a retail story, make sure it's simple, has a beginning, middle and end (as covered in the previous

Your customers don't care about your products or service. They care about themselves, their dreams, their goals. Now, they will care much more if you help them reach their goals, and to do that you must understand their goals as well as their needs and deepest desires.

Steve Jobs

chapter) and, again, that you can tell it in two minutes or less. Your own retail story is about *why* you guys are still around and why anyone should care. If you are an independent, make sure your story is about you or your family and your personal *why*. If you own or manage a franchise store, or you're part of a larger retail group, tell a tiny bit about the larger group but make a connection between your organisation and your personality.

And if you are part of a larger organisation, don't shy away from becoming the champion of your store. This doesn't have to be something you advertise with your head office, but stepping up and making sure you've got a well-told story about your *why* and your passion helps customers, suppliers and other partners know why they should be working and purchasing with you.

If you solely own your business, then by all means make sure your story is on your website and everywhere.

The previous chapter outlined the basic three-part structure of a good story. Now, here's a quick five-step snapshot for how to turn a good story into a great story:

1   *Remember your hero:* Put a picture next to your notepad or computer of who your hero is as a reminder. As you go through each of the following steps, constantly refer back to how they would feel about your story.

2   *Paint the picture:* Set the scene and describe events leading up to starting your retail venture (or perhaps the events leading up to when the originators did).

3   *Use vivid and emotive language to describe your story:* If possible, when revealing other characters or situations, try to give people a visual of what people were like or what they sounded like. (And, sure, do an impersonation!)

4   *Set up the turning point of the story:* What was life like before and what was the catalyst that set everything into action? Did you decide to move into retail because of economic, political or personal strife, or did the planets align? Describe this.

5   *Always end with a moral or a takeaway message:* End with your reason for why you do what you do – for example, to help your customer, families or the environment. Or provide a clear takeaway message – such as to never give up on your dreams.

For inspiration, have a look at my story at retailrockstars.com.au/about-us and notice how my hero is the retailer. How did I set the stage, what was the turning point and the moral takeaway?

Your story is critical; it can be told to suppliers, customers, employees and other businesses. The story is what intrigues people, and this is how people remember you and your store over time. It reminds them why they should shop, work and do business with you.

People remember a good story – but they don't always remember a store.

 ## TIME OUT: WRITING YOUR RETAIL STORY IN 10 MINUTES (PLUS ONE MEETING)

Follow these steps to draft your personal retail story and your company story:

1   Set your phone's timer to five minutes and use the five-step snapshot process outlined earlier in this chapter to draft your personal retail story. So first, paint a picture, and then jot down some characters and facts and the kinds of descriptive and emotive words you can use to capture these and perhaps inject humour. Next, briefly describe what your life was like before owning the store and what your turning point was. Finally, include your moral or takeaway. Outline a story that you would present to staff and remember – don't overthink this; simple is best.

2   Now, set your phone's timer for another five minutes and refine your story by first putting all the four points together, then by writing them into a short – under two minutes, spoken – flowing story about how you came to own or manage your store. Test yourself – do you have a moral or takeaway message? Are all the ingredients there?

3   Now, schedule a meeting with three to four other staff and/or managers. Quickly describe the five steps to storytelling and ask them to brainstorm a company story in the next twenty-four to forty-eight hours. Compare notes, collaborate ideas and create a story for your company. Make sure everyone who works for you knows and memorises this story. Make this story part of inducting new staff and suppliers.

Now that you've got your personal story and your company story down pat, think about other areas you can use this powerful tool in. This same process can be used during events, or when explaining changes in staffing or commission rates – you name it. So start writing down and refining stories for those areas too. Before you know it, you'll be using stories like a pro.

One final tip – make sure all your staff know how to tell familiar product and lifestyle stories for customers, along with additional micro stories that help with cross-selling or aid in other ways with sales. But also highlight how staff can use stories to communicate with suppliers and other local businesses.

TELLING A STORY VISUALLY WITHIN YOUR STORE

While visual merchandising isn't my area of expertise, I've included some information on it here as an aid to your overall customer experience and also as you help customers imagine possible scenarios right within your store. Because, at the end of the day, we've all got plenty of products on display. If you're just going to stack them up and arrange them by colour, then where's the story or intrigue in that? Our endgame in visual storytelling is to inspire a customer to think about new possibilities and to help them explore what it might be like to adopt that new lifestyle or activity. A great visual story will take the customer on a journey of discovery. Whether they purchase or not, the seed has been planted once they've explored the display.

When I first started my customer experience experiment, I concentrated primarily on events and workshops inside our store. Initially, we didn't have access to emailing our customers or even a local Facebook page, so one of our biggest challenges was getting the word out for upcoming workshops and educational shows. We had an upcoming workshop led by a local nutritionist who was presenting information on nutrient loading. (This was a fascinating take on getting three times the daily recommended intake of vitamins and minerals, and how efficient your body and organs become while being flooded with these vitamins and minerals.)

To set up for the workshop, we used an island benchtop in our showroom as the backdrop and created a beautiful setting. I also went out and bought a large 'bouquet' of kale and other assorted 'super-foods' and put them in a large vase in the middle of the table. Each setting in this area of the store had recipes for smoothies and turmeric lattes and other assorted high-nutrient treats – along with invitations to the upcoming 'nutrient-dense workshop'.

I noticed quite a few people stopping and looking at the table and snapping off pictures of our lovely display. When the date for the workshop came, we were oversubscribed and I had a waiting list of ten additional people wanting a seat. And not only was the workshop heavily attended but also over 70 per cent of the people attending that day walked out with either a new blender or some type of accessory our expert was using.

As retailers, merchandising is something we all do. But when we slap together a bunch of products without a story it barely gets noticed. To create a visual story that means something and draws attention inside your store you need to review the five-step snapshot for telling stories and just tweak it a bit for visual storytelling:

1 *Remember your hero:* When promoting or telling a story through visual merchandising, take five minutes out first to determine *who* your hero really is. Are they trendy, sporty, thrifty, a lil' bit geeky?

2 *Paint the picture:* Set the scene and describe what the hero is trying to achieve; are they after fame, love, entertainment, health? What would be their motivation? In my example in this section, my customers and ideal attendees were after optimum health but were also a bit on trend, and probably liked exercising or yoga. So I hung some yoga mats on the back of the chairs. You want to include things in your story that will grab their attention and make them say, 'Hey, that looks like something I'd like over there.'

3 *Use vivid and emotive language to describe your story:* For my situation, I wanted to highlight our expert, so I placed several of her books on the benchtop that had her biography and credentials on it.

4 *Set up the turning point of the story:* Here, if possible, try to point out what customers might miss out on. In my example, we had symptom cards that were given to me by the nutritionist. These had symptoms of what being deficient in magnesium looked like for example. I used these cards as decorations around each place setting.

5 *Always end with a moral or a takeaway message:* End with your reason for why you do what you do. In my example, our takeaway was the workshop, and so I placed invites with how to RSVP all over the table that people could take away.

As you can see, a lot of similarities exist between verbally telling a story and merchandising one. Probably the most important part of both, however, is to plan and have a few moments to think about your hero and what you want to convey to them before you start grabbing products and getting too carried away.

Customers may forget the last discount you gave them or your recent ad campaign, but they'll never forget how you made them feel at an event inside your store.

Amy Roche (yes, that's me!)

Part VII

EVENTS: BEST-KEPT SECRET FOR RETAIL

STRATEGY FIVE: IN-STORE EVENTS

Now, I know what you're thinking. I mean I'm a businessperson, I've been a global and national marketer, and I always considered events and event marketing a bit, well, 'woo-woo'. So I get it, I really do but just stick with me for a bit. After all, you've come this far right?

In this tech-crazed, hyper-competitive industry we live in, you need all the help you can get, and events have proven – not just to me in my Experiment but also to many other big brands and industries – to be a genuine game-changer.

In fact, according to Live Marketing, 67 per cent of B2B content marketers consider event marketing to be their most effective strategy – and no wonder when brands see that 84 per cent of consumers repurchase a product promoted at an event.

Events can build deep and meaningful connections with your customers. I'm not talking here about the kind of connections you worry about now – the ones you're not sure will help you make your budget this month – but the more profitable and meaningful connections for you, your customers and your staff.

As we learned in chapter 3, emotionally connected customers can not only be a lot more fun to work with, but also work hard to advocate how awesome you are to others. In that chapter, I run through the benefits highly engaged customers (HECs) can bring to your retail business, including stronger loyalty, great advocacy and increased opportunity for upselling and cross-selling. (Refer to chapter 3 for the specifics of these benefits.) And events are the perfect way to create and retain these HECs, as you build trust and appreciation. The following chapters explain further.

EVENTS PACK
A PUNCH

16

At the end of the day, we all want engaged customers because it's a lot more fun and more profitable to work with them. They will appreciate your unique approach and love you even more for sharing it with them. But, as you can imagine, if engaging your customers were easy, every retailer would be doing it.

As you are all too aware, retail is a very busy business to run. To add to the confusion and 'busyness', our customers are also crazy busy. Engaging people in this 'busy' state of mind is hard work, so how can we cut through and *wake up* these disengaged, price-sensitive and sometimes fickle customers? You guessed it – events!

> Traditional marketing has become less effective in breaking down people's defence mechanisms. Face-to-face has become the best way to create chemistry and engagement.
>
> *Kerry Smith*

THE POWER BEHIND EVENTS

People are more open today than even just ten years ago to forming closer bonds with a brand. This is one of the reasons inspirational and educational events are so powerful for retailers. There's never been a better time, or better market conditions, to start driving this new trend within retail. Helping your customers solve meaningful problems and connecting with their emotional versus logic-only (features and benefits) sides can be a powerful engagement tool.

The in-store experience you create can help your customers feel at ease in your store, better understand your products and can also connect their lifestyle goals with your brand.

All the top advisory firms – like Deloitte, PWC and KPMG – have been using events to engage their customers and attract new ones for well over ten years. But with the top end of town using their own experts as well as partnering with others, it's no wonder the area still seems like some sort of secret. Events are just as powerful on a smaller scale, however. Sure, a retailer's events will vary in nature from something put on by Deloitte, but the premise remains the same – we too are looking to forge relationships, build trust and, of course, bring new sales and customers on board.

For those with a bit of lingering doubt out there, the following provides some outside expertise and figures to show the power and sheer size of events. Note that, if required, I've taken events like sporting events and festivals, which may have significant brand influences going on, out of these figures and just focused on B2B and B2C events that are hosted by business. Here's how powerful events are around the world:

- According to the *UK Economic Impact Study 2013*, in the UK £33.3 billion was spent by businesses on events such as exhibitions, trade fairs and corporate events. This was out of £39.1 billion spent in total in the events sector (which included the music and sporting events).

- In the US, in business events alone, over 1.8 million business events are held each year, which equates to over US$280 billion in spending. Indeed, meetings and events contribute more to the US GDP than the air transportation, motion picture, sound recording, performing arts and spectator sports industries.[1]

- And in Australia, in the 2013–14 financial year, over 37 million people attended more than 412,000 business events[2] – and these figures are on the rise.

- According to the US Bureau of Labor Statistics, in the ten years from 2010 to 2020, conventions and events are expected to expand by 44 per cent, outpacing any other industry.

So events are big business – but, as I said, they can be great for small businesses too (or big businesses who want to look smaller and more local). They don't have to involve big bucks and fancy function centres – as I've already mentioned, you have an existing function centre right on your shop floor. In fact, in my opinion, events can be even more effective for smaller businesses like individual retailers than they are for big firms. Bigger businesses are expected to pull out all stops and really razzle and dazzle their clients. Whereas when local businesses put on events, especially free ones, it's my experience that customers are not expecting the Queen to attend with fireworks at the end. If executed well, even the most humble gathering can actually move and inspire people more than big events because it's a more intimate environment. Events work best when they bring your local people together, humanise your business and create massive engagement. Pretty amazing, right?

EVENTS CAN DISRUPT HABITS

Shopping habits are an interesting phenomenon in retail – depending on which side you're on with a customer. The habits customers (and potential customers) have established can either be a help or a hindrance. Let me explain. We know that when a shopper is in the habit of shopping with you, it's great and you're happy. In our busy, stressed-out lives, we tend to be somewhat creatures of habit. But if you're trying to reach out to a new customer who's never shopped with you before, it can take quite a bit of convincing – and this is where events are most powerful.

See, we like to keep to what we know. Just think about the easiest and most repetitive shopping we all do – groceries. Research says most consumers shop at the same grocery store the majority of the time. We know where the items that we like are, we know what brands they carry and we also are familiar with their store layout.

When we move away from the known into the unknown, we usually feel a small amount of unease. You may not be aware of the uneasiness, but rest assured it's there, and it's what keeps us shopping at the same familiar places – until something disrupts that habit.

So if you have an existing stressed-out customer – life's pretty easy. Keep doing what you're doing, either about the same or slightly better, and you'll keep them coming back. But if you're looking at attracting people to a new store environment, you might be up for a bigger challenge depending on your industry.

But when you start hosting events inside your store, you open up several really powerful disruptors:

- Inviting people into your store for a valuable experience means you are triggering the 'reciprocity rule' – that is, the rules that say when someone gives you something you feel obligated to give something back. What event attendees 'give back' might just be their purchase of the next thing they need that you sell, or it might be something they buy on the day of the event. Either way, you're getting an opportunity.

- You're putting them in complete control to choose an event that resonates with them – and remember stressed customers like to be in control.

- If they had a positive psychological experience inside your store, they've now associated your store with that positive experience. Again, this is another opportunity – either on the day or later – and you've got a whole lotta positives going on.

In the following chapter, I go into the specifics of what type of event to plan and when – for now, let's have another quick reminder of why experience wins over price.

MOVING AWAY FROM YOUR GIFT OF PRICE AND TOWARD EXPERIENCE AND EVENTS

While customers today may seem more fickle, in many cases it's self-inflicted. Our obsession with sales, pricing and product within the 'sales machine' doesn't differentiate us in the best way. Perhaps you even ran similar promotions to what we did at my store, where we had to encourage our customers initially to shop online by giving them incentives, cash-back bonuses and special pricing. So, whether you trained them yourself or allowed your competitors to do so, shopping for price and discounts is now a top-of-mind action for consumers. Price is important, but it doesn't have to be your only story.

In the same spirit of how we encouraged them to shop online, you can now invite them back into the store. Once there, however, we do need to make sure we can show off our personalities, our strengths and our genuine interest in making their lives easier, more productive or healthier. They need to see, hear and feel our retail story and feel like they are part of something more than just a store with more 'stuff' in it.

When it comes to winning over a customer by price alone, only one retailer will ever win that battle, and that will be the one who makes the least on the deal. So don't set yourself up for that kind of failure. You must instead start focusing on delivering events and experiences inside your store that cannot be price-matched and cannot be copied because they are unique to your store and served up individually by you and your staff or team of experts for your special kind of customer.

Just recently Nike opened up a flagship store in Soho that boasted, among many other things, 'smart' treadmills that capture people's running stats, a soccer trial zone and a half-basketball court. So the future of retail experience is already here and happening. Nike stores all over the world have events already – check out their Nike Running Club, for example, which is already up and running (wink wink) in Sydney and Melbourne. In Sydney, for instance, they have the Nike Training Club and hold free classes on strength and mobility training right inside the store. In New York, the Nike Running Club is sometimes hosted by WRU, which stands for We Run Uptown – a local group of running lovers. So Nike as a retailer is already making community connections and allowing those communities to bring their brand to life. They are not curating the entire experience from start to finish.

In a similar move, Adidas focuses on experiences in its own new flagship store, but the experiences and the events Adidas offers are, of course, unique to Adidas. What's clear going forward is that events and in-store experiences are the future of real-life engagement with customers. Make sure you're the first off the block to start experimenting with what your customers need from you. Get in early and start refining those ideas and make your competitors play catch-up with you. Even if your head office isn't leading the way just yet, you can locally be providing these amazing experiences for your customers today. And trust me – if you have the success we did, you'll have retail store owners and others asking what your secret is.

Keep your competitors at arm's length by making them battle for the lowest price day in and day out with the other slowly adapting retailers. The day will come when your competitors wake up to the experience and events revolution – and when they do, that's fine too because by then you'll have your own unique experiences that can't be matched anywhere.

TIME OUT: SEARCH OUT GREAT EXPERIENCES AROUND YOU

It's time to do a little market research and experience searching. Start out by Googling your industry and upcoming events. For instance, if you are in the camping or adventure retailing industry, start looking for brands or retailers who are already hosting events. If you can't find any, start searching under top-notch brands and retailers in the UK, the US or Canada.

Next, think of the last really fun and memorable event you attended – what were the best bits of it? Reflect on how they scored in the following areas:

- *Human-to-human experience:* Was this a face-to-face event or virtual? What were the benefits of that?

- *Easy to communicate and share socially:* Was this something you wanted to share with friends? Did you take pictures even if you don't use social media personally?

- *All about you:* Did you feel they made a fuss of you? How could they have done things better?

- *Advocacy:* Did you feel compelled to tell others about your experience or book in for another experience or event?

- *Community and cause:* Did you feel many of the people who were there were like you in some way? How could the organisers really tap into that?

- *Returns and benefits:* What did you get out of it? Why would you go back?

Your answers to the preceding questions can give you great insight into how your customers feel, so keep them close and glean from them when creating your own unique experiences for customers.

So if you're convinced, let's get into the crux of providing and hosting events and experiences in-store, and how you can track their effectiveness to get your engagement, loyalty and trust working overtime.

EVENTS: BRINGING IT ALL TOGETHER

17

If we are looking to 'house' all the parts of this book together and tie them up with a neat bow, the best way to use all of these powerful strategies together is inside an event.

Events can be carefully constructed bits of emotional engagement – in one swoop, they can help you to:

- deliver a face-to-face live event with your customers that really humanises your store – covering humanics

- move away from focusing on price only towards delivering unique experiences – becoming more than a sales machine and offering experiential retailing

- share facts and spread the word about special events, facts and product experiences through stories – covering retail storytelling

> Good fortune is what happens when opportunity meets with planning.
>
> *Thomas Edison*

- measure your events through technology and reports, making sure your events yield returns for your retail store – covering event mechanics (coming later in this chapter).

DIGGING DEEPER: HOW TO FIND EVENT IDEAS FOR CUSTOMERS

Have you ever run an event within your store? One that truly connects with your customers, creates deeper engagement and creates opportunities for more business?

If you have, you know that, while a bit of planning is involved, once they are scheduled and working the event becomes its own 'experience machine'. Kind of like what I describe in chapter 6, the event starts working its own cycle, becoming something talked about, something celebrated and definitely something to be proud of.

If you haven't run an in-store event, there has probably never been a better time to get started, given everything that we've been talking about in this book. To help with your planning, the following brings together many of the ideas covered throughout the book:

- Arrange specialised events in your store that help curate the decision-making process for customers. Remember – your customers today are stressed and overwhelmed, so make it easy for them. And, of course, providing tips and product information is even better if it doesn't come from you!

- Provide compelling reasons to break habits and routine if your target audience is not your existing customers. Offer free workshops through lifestyle websites, local community boards and gyms, and establish some value-added business partnerships locally.

- Partner with local trusted experts, such as bloggers, coaches and other real-life experts who legitimately use or work with your products. Don't make your customers sort through the confusion – too much choice just adds to their stress.

Remember – events are all about providing your customers with a human connection, and this can extend into other areas as well, as you try to get people to shop more often with you in-store. For example, if customers purchase online for in-store pickup, make sure when they are in-store you invite them to your next event or give them a special number to call if they have problems with the product. Reach out to them; don't just hand over the product. Make the most of that personal interaction.

This same idea applies when you have a first-time customer in your store – make sure you reach out to them and invite them to your next event experience.

Now, let's put everything you've uncovered through the book together – this will involve reviewing some of the findings from your 'Time out' sessions in earlier chapters. Here's how to focus in on your unique type of event and how you should run it:

1   Review what you identified in our localisation and humanics exercises (in the chapters in part IV) and create an in-store event topic that resonates with your local customers. Remember – go niche and specific rather than trying to capture every customer in one event. Do quick customer surveys (using something like Survey Monkey) to get an idea of your customers' unique interests and goals.

2   Determine whether you need to source a local educator or expert who can present value. If so, who?

3   Define your event story (review what makes a good story – see the chapters in part VI).

4   Communicate your event story, via technology platforms, email, social media and local press.

5   Select a platform(s) to promote your event and gather RSVPs if needed (more on this in the following section).

6   Use this event to engage and 'wake up' existing customers and bring new more engaged ones in.

And a tip on choosing experts: always make sure you vet your experts well. This is something I've built into my training program because it can require a bit of extra work, but at the very least make sure they have their own business, you've heard them speak, and they have a unique way of solving problems or getting results.

When I first started offering events in my store, I always began vetting experts by reviewing their written information – like a book, e-book, website, social media or brochure. If that sounded interesting, I'd ask them where they were speaking next and I'd attend to hear them.

EVENT MECHANICS

Events can't work in isolation. One of the most important things about running an event is the mechanics of how it all works together. How do you plan, develop, manage and report on events that work and yield returns for your retail store? Event mechanics is how everything works together, and is about the insights and data gathered before, during and after the event. It combines the data and tech so you can apply it to future events and make adaptations, based on insights gathered, to grow your engagement with customers even further.

Remember that you need to get your customers out of 'sleep-walking' mode and disrupt their habits. Mechanics are the tools that help you communicate, capture, nurture and 'wake up' your customer so that they genuinely want to do more business with you.

Utilising event mechanics will help you create events that are memorable for your audience, but only if they have the correct structure. So how do you implement and use them?

Just as you'd measure your slow-moving stock or sales against previous weeks, events also need to be measured and tracked for effectiveness. Event mechanics need to capture who's attending and who's buying, as well as what's working and what's not. As they say, what gets measured gets done, and you can use some simple hacks for managing events with technology. In my experience, each retailer uses their own POS (point of sale) system, and they all work in different ways and have their own set of challenges and advantages. I'm not an IT expert, nor do I expect you to change systems that your whole company uses. What's most important is having a way to communicate with your new communities. If your hands are tied and you're unable to send EDMs (emails) to your customers, I'd suggest finding a way to do this. My clients who can't email utilise my company to do this; alternatively, if you're not going to get in too much trouble, you can always start up a free MailChimp account to start out with. This list needs to be constantly updated with new attendees at the very minimum and can be used to communicate with customers before and after the event.

Always make sure you take RSVPs, because this pre-gathers information and also helps you know when to cut numbers off. Heaps of free programs are available, especially if you decide not to charge for your events – for example, I've used both Eventbrite and Sticky Tickets. I'd suggest initially making your events free until they are routinely booked out or overbooked. I know what you're thinking – it's what other retailers I talk to also think. No doubt you think you're never going to have to cut off numbers because no-one will come. Trust me; you'll begin filling your workshops and events with little or no effort.

After each event or experience, make sure you find a way to match up customer data with that of your attendees. In the beginning, this can seem like a very manual process; however, once you have a process set up, find an admin assistant or someone who can routinely match up your customer data with that of the attendees.

While digital surveys are all the rage, I found the absolute best indicator of success is to have a concise survey for attendees to fill out then and there. This too will give you an indication if they've shopped with you before and what interests they might have.

Again, purchases are tracked with whatever POS system you have, and most systems can pull data on a voucher or special offer codes, and it's here you can find some short cuts and evaluate which events are producing the best results.

SCHEDULING OF EXPERIENCES IN YOUR STORE

Just like many other facets of your business, there are times to educate, times to inspire, times to focus on product and times to just have some good ol' fun with your customers.

Working out how much time to give each area is a delicate balance of time available, cost and emphasis. I like to have in-store events and experiences at least once a month but, if you can manage it, once a week or fortnight is even better. Based on this minimum number, I use a tidy and easy way to plan out events in-store. This by no means is meant to stifle your creativity, but the most effective plans are those that are scheduled and communicated regularly with staff, suppliers and customers.

Based on the Experiment in our store, the best mix of events and experiences for customers that resulted in the highest outcomes regarding attendance and sales was realised by following the 40/30/20/10 (for education/inspire/product/fun) rule.

You should be predominantly helping and serving your customers most of the time. I think education should be everyone's go-to – it says you care and also helps you keep on the pulse of what is happening trend-wise. Education and working with other entrepreneurs and experts can help you with more than just customer engagement, for example – it can lead to changes in your product range, help options, the education of your sales teams and more.

An example of what the following events and experiences might look like is as follows:

- *Education:* These are workshops and educational seminars for your customers. They teach high-value and niched information. Many times, these classes or workshops might include a free e-book, a checklist or some printouts.

- *Inspiration:* These might be style guides and shows with experts or members of your team. Rather than being solely focused on education, these will be predominately about giving ideas and showing off new trends and your store's thought leadership – so show off your expertise and industry knowledge here. These could also be self-help type experiences where your customer is taken through a journey and inspired to take action.

- *Product:* These can be either inspirational or educational but have a heavy emphasis on a particular type of product. For instance, you might get a particular supplier to fund this. In the past, I've held these types of events with suppliers like Breville, and we showcased several different products and what you could specifically make and do with them. Or you can showcase a particular type of product and show aspects of what's out there and what works best for certain jobs.

- *Fun:* The sky is the limit here. We've had many of these, and they have ranged from superhero days – where all the staff dress up as their favourite superhero, and we've had kids and parents (customers) enter best costume awards – to lots of fun charity days, cycling competitions and cooking competitions. My husband and I have Irish heritage, so we always had a big St Paddy's day celebration – which the staff and the customers all liked. This is really about showcasing you and your uniqueness and having fun with it.

So, if you're looking to experiment yourself, start out with a minimum commitment of once-a-month events in-store and use the 40/30/20/10 rule. This looks something like this:

- educate – 40 per cent, or for about five to six months of the year

- inspire – 30 per cent, or for three to four months out of the year

- how-to and product specifics – 20 per cent, or for two months out of the year
- just be silly and have fun – 10 per cent, or for one month of the year.

Obviously, these figures don't come out exact, so you'll need to adjust based on your personal retail product and customer and how often you'd like to start producing these experiences. As an example, for several of my clients, I increased educational events to being held six times each year, three events for inspiring, two for how-to's and one for fun.

No absolutes exist here, but what I'd say is that identifying and really knowing your customer and what they suffer or need help with will guide your own events and experience ratios.

The point to this is not to have an exact prescription, but to acknowledge that you need to add value to your customers in different ways, recognising your own unique customer and their needs.

And remember – experiential is counterintuitive for retailers. While you might want to make product-specific and how-to events the dominant area, remember the deposits and withdrawals metaphor with your customers. The majority of customers are tired of being 'sold to', so after trialling different ratios ourselves and gathering up surveys, we found this was a perfect mix for many of our retail clients.

So now it's time to get started in your store and have some fun!

RETAIL REVIVAL

I'll keep this brief because hopefully by now you're champing at the bit to make some changes in-store and I encourage you to do this straight away, while it's still fresh.

While it's lovely that you've read my book, what I really want is for you to start getting some wins on the board. I want you to start crushing that 'sales machine' mentality, start utilising more customer-centric ideas and experiment to make a name for yourself locally.

Maybe you're wondering why I want you to succeed so badly. Because several years ago now, while blessed with a great store and brand, I felt I wasn't in control of my own destiny. I bought retail books and began researching but felt all the advice was on *big* things I couldn't change. So my retail journey

> If your customers are made to feel as if they are outsiders, they will eventually find a competitor who makes them feel better about doing business with them.
>
> *Shep Hyken*

has brought me full circle to helping other store owners and managers turn their stores around and gain back control in ways where they can make a huge difference. While I loved owning a retail store, I find it even more rewarding to help out other retailers now. I know what it feels like when you're not in control of your own destiny. But, as I've shown you, if I can make these changes and turn around my store so can you.

I'd like nothing more than to get an email from you in two months' time with a story about how your head office has called, wanting to know what in the hell you're doing to turn things around so quickly. Your customer-retention is high, sales are up and profitability is finally on the mend. I'm in it for the retailer who might be a bit under the thumb, who is talented yet under-resourced, who, despite all the generic ideas your head office throws at you, still gets up every day and turns the lights on in the shop. (Okay – most days?)

If your head is hanging low from all the Amazon talk and the retailer bashing you've heard in the news lately – don't listen to it and don't watch it. It's rubbish. Retail is alive and well, and if you start to reach out and connect with your local customers, they will start noticing you and shopping with you.

A LITTLE ON THE FUTURE OF RETAIL

Historically, I think this era will be recorded as a major reckoning for retail. Those retailers who get it, who adapt their stores and, more importantly, their mindsets will live on; those who don't will suffer.

Look, I'm not a futurist, but I'm a retailer, a marketer and someone who's very curious about issues facing retail at the moment – I wish we could all succeed, but we won't.

While we've been talking about the customer experience for nearly ten years now, many times people and companies still imply experience relates to the 'look' of the brand experience – to enhance the experience, you can just change this look. But it's not about changing your logo, creating an app or a new design. It's roll-up-your-sleeves hard work. It's about getting your brand promise right and making that customer experience part of what your business is now and is all about.

This is not something you can simply hire out to the top agency in town – the change needs to be personal and needs the full attention of retail leaders. It's not going to be easy, but it's not rocket science either. You'll need to dig deep, talk with your customers, distil their responses and find answers to how you're going to deliver unique experiences for your unique area and customers. How can you help them more efficiently, and differently? How can you make money other than selling products?

Retailers need to re-envision what their stores will look like in the future and start experimenting and working towards that now. Small retail events will give you big insights into what people need and want from you. It's better to start experimenting with individual locations and small budgets than to go into full-blown national campaigns that could be off the mark and lead to a budget blowout or, even worse, a PR nightmare.

You know how fast-paced retail is – you live in it. I can't stress enough the importance of just getting started right away. When I started writing this book, many people laughed at my event and experimenting ideas and that was only three years ago. Don't wait for someone else to invent what your customers need now – start testing, measuring and delivering those magical moments today.

Physical stores of the future will also start shifting from being a dirty liability to the absolute best asset and anchor of a brand – shifting away from being a product distribution house for click-and-collect to more of a media powerhouse where all things originate from. Showcasing and experiencing new products and the lifestyles that accompany them, as well as the experiences that go with or enhance the people who use those products.

In essence, rather than being the *product* distribution house, physical locations will be the distributors of *experiences*.

Like-minded people will gather there for shared and personalised products, learning and enrichment. In a few short years, I think we'll also start to see changes in how retailers make money. Brands and interested parties will see stores as another platform for new product release and a place that stocks their product stories.

I sincerely hope that I have inspired you enough to realise that our customers have forever changed and will continue to do so, and that at the very heart of a great retailer is a closet psychologist noticing subtle changes and differences, and adapting along the way.

Personally, I can't wait for the future of retail, and my only hope is that I hear from you and your staff about all the success you've had at educating and wooing your customers in your own unique way – and about how much fun you're all having while doing it.

Seriously, don't be a stranger – reach out and connect with me through my website or on LinkedIn (www.linkedin.com/in/amyroche1). And best of luck!

ABOUT THE AUTHOR

Amy Roche is a retailer, marketer and in-store customer experience advocate with a passion for helping retailers reconnect and engage with their local customers.

She's been in the retail and marketing industry in both Australia and the US for 20 years, owning a 2500m^2 retail store for 11 years in Brisbane. Amy is now a keynote presenter and author, and the director of Retail Rockstars – a retail marketing platform that sources experts, and manages, markets and creates LIVE in-store events for retailers' customers (www.retailrockstars.com.au).

From Chicago, Amy has lived in Brisbane, Australia since 2002 with her husband Dale, and children, Harrison, Conor and Ailish, along with Rio the dog and 'kitty' the cat.

ACKNOWLEDGEMENTS

Who would have thought writing a book while running your own business and family would be so challenging for everyone involved – and rewarding at the same time.

I would like to thank my friends who encouraged me and inspired me when I really needed it. You've played a huge role in getting this book finished and have also helped my fellow comrades in retail at a very trying time.

Thank you to the special people who have supported me for years as I researched and sometimes procrastinated in more books and papers than I care to admit: my good mate Lisa Cutforth, James Brockhurst and writing mentor Andrew Griffiths – without you, the idea of this book would have never made it out of my head.

Thank you also to the very special people at KPI (Key Person of Influence) for always pushing me and instilling in me to keep GSD (getting shit done) – in particular, a special mention to Glen Carlson for his words of wisdom and advice over the past three years.

Also, my heartfelt gratitude to The Good Guys and specifically other JVPs who believed in me and encouraged me and wanted to be part of my crazy ideas and events. We had something very special, and I still call many of you great friends today.

Thank you to my kids – Lil' Harrison, Ailish and Conor – who put up with my shut office door, writing deadlines and all kinds of other inconveniences that kids shouldn't have to put up with.

Thank you to my wonderful husband, Dale Vincent Roche, my partner in crime and overall amazing man – somehow you managed to keep all the balls up in the air while I wrote this book and I love you dearly for your patience and encouragement.

Last but not least, a very big thank you to you the reader – the retailer – for taking a chance on reading a book written by a first-time author. I'll never take your action for granted and have a tonne of gratitude. Thank you for inviting me and my ideas into your retail world.

Hoping your in-store experience is a smashing success!

Amy

NOTES

Chapter 1

1   Mindframe National Media Initiative, sourced by the Australian Health Department on www.mindframe-media.info/for-media/reporting-mental-illness/facts-and-stats

2   Gallup's Negative Experience Index 2013 components, cited in www.gallup.com/poll/171419/world-becoming-slightly-negative.aspx.

3   APS Stress and Wellbeing Survey found on http://www.psychology.org.au/psychologyweek/survey/results-stress-and-wellbeing.

4   Allan V Horowitz and Jerome C Wakefield, 'Our New Era of Anxiety', Salon, June 2, 2012, www.salon.com/2012/06/02/our_new_era_of_anxiety.

5   Duke University, 'Brain sets prices with emotional value.' ScienceDaily, 3 July 2013, www.sciencedaily.com/releases/2013/07/130702173156.htm.

6   William Poundstone, *Priceless: The Myth of Fair Value*, New York: Hill and Wang, 2011.

7   Kit Yarrow, *Decoding the New Consumer Mind*, San Francisco: Jossey-Bass 2014.

8   Christopher J Carpenter, 'A Meta-Analysis of the Effectiveness of the "But You Are Free" Compliance-Gaining Technique', *Communication Studies* 64, no. 1 (2013): 6–17.

9   Kit Yarrow, *op. cit.*

10 Torsten Bornemann and Christian Homburg, 'Psychological Distance and Due Role of Price', *Journal of Consumer Research* 38, no. 3 (October 2011): 490–504.

11 Kit Yarrow, *op. cit.*

12 Kit Yarrow, *op. cit.*

13 Gartner Webinars, 'By 2017 the CMO will spend more on IT than the CIO', Jan 3, 2012, mygartner.com.

14 AARP The Magazine, *Loneliness among Older Adults*, 2010, assets.aarp.org/rgcenter/general/loneliness_2010.pdf.

15 Australian Institute of Family Studies, 'Cohabitation 2013', aifs.gov.au/facts-and-figures/living-together-australia.

16 Ron Duclos, Echo Wen Wan, and Yuwei Jiang, 'Show Me the Honey: Effects of Social Exclusion on Financial Risk Taking', *Journal of Consumer Research* 40, no 1 (2013): 122–135.

17 2017 Edelman Trust Barometer, www.edelman.com/trust2017.

18 David Brooks, 'What Our Words Tell Us', *New York Times*, 20 May 2013.

19 2017 Edelman Trust Barometer, *op. cit.*

20 Jeremy Dean, 'Twitter: 10 Psychological Insights', PsyBlog, 10 August 2010, www.spring.org.uk/2010/08/twitter-10-psychological-insights.php.

Chapter 2

1   NAB retail figures from 2016; business.nab.com.au/nab-online-retail-sales-index-june-2016-17897.

2   Google, 'Digital Impact on In-Store Shopping: Research Debunks Common Myths', 2014, www.thinkwithgoogle.com/research-studies/digital-impact-on-in-store-shopping.html.

3　Roy Morgan Research, '"Experiences" over "things": Aussies spending more on leisure and entertainment, but less on discretionary commodities', www.roymorgan.com.au/ findings/7064-experiences-over-things-aussies-spending-more-on-leisure-entertainment-201611241252.

Chapter 3

1　Rosetta Consulting, 'The Economics of Engagement: Quantifying the Link between Engagement and Growth', currents.rosetta. com/2015/07/the-economics-of-engagement-quantifying-the-link-between-engagement-and-growth.

Chapter 11

1　2017 Edelman Trust Barometer, www.edelman.com/trust2017.

2　Westpac media releases, 'Aussies support Australian by shopping local', 23 January 2015, www.westpac.com.au/about-westpac/ media/media-releases/2015/23-january.

Chapter 12

1　Steve McClellan, 'Kids to marketers: We want tech gadgets, not toys' *MediaDailyNews*, 13 March 2013, mediapost.com/ publications/article/195747.

2　Initially cited by Abraham Maslow, 'A Theory of Human Motivation', 1943. (Carl Rogers coined the term 'self-actualisation'.)

Chapter 14

1　Based on research available at www.sarahdoody.com/what-science-says-about-the-effect-of-stories-on-our-brains/#. WDPZreF95R0

Chapter 16

1   Meeting Professionals International, 'Meeting and Event Industry Facts', www.mpiweb.org/docs/default-source/move-forward/moveforward_industryfacts-2015.pdf.

2   Business Events Council of Australia, 'The Value of Business Events to Australia', February 2015, www.businesseventscouncil.org.au/files/View_Report.pdf.

INTERESTED IN MORE?

Get in touch with Amy via the following:

- Join the conversation and reach out at www.linkedin.com/in/amyroche1.

- Find more out about The Retail Experiment, workshops, events and references at theretailexperiment.com.au.

- For retail blogs, checklists and all kinds of helpful stuff for retailers, visit retailrockstars.com.au.

CPSIA information can be obtained
at www.ICGtesting.com
Printed in the USA
BVOW06s1647211117
501000BV00014B/691/P